D1557125

a book of variations
love – zygal – art facts

bpNichol
edited by Stephen Voyce

Coach House Books, Toronto

AURORA PUBLIC LIBRARY

copyright © Eleanor Nichol, for the estate of bpNichol, 2013
foreword © Stephen Voyce, 2013

love: a book of remembrances was published by Talonbooks in 1974.
zygal: a book of mysteries and translations was published by Coach House
    Press in 1985 and reissued by Coach House Books in 2003.
art facts: a book of contexts was published by Chax Press in 1990.

  Canada

Coach House Books thanks, for their support, the Block Grant Programs of the
Canada Council for the Arts and the Ontario Arts Council. We also appreciate
the support of the Government of Canada through the Canada Book Fund.

LIBRARY AND ARCHIVES CANADA CATALOGUING IN PUBLICATION

Nichol, B. P., 1944-1988
        A book of variations : Love ; Zygal ; Art facts / bpNichol ; edited by
Stephen Voyce.

ISBN 978-1-55245-272-1

        I. Voyce, Stephen, 1978- II. Title. III. Title: Love. IV. Title: Art facts. V.
Title: Zygal.

PS8527.I32B66 2013   C811'.54   C2013-900261-8

Contents

Foreword
by Stephen Voyce

> 'Because most people stop at the Z
> But not me!'
> —Dr. Seuss, *On Beyond Zebra!*

bpNichol's work oscillates between poetry, prose, music, comics, collaborative performance art, visual art, mixed media and new media. He wrote novels and children's books, screenplays and sound scores, short stories and an epic poem. Even his concrete verse moves between the hand-drawn, typewritten and typeset variety. His influences include Gertrude Stein and Dick Tracy, Dada and Dr. Seuss. He was a gifted editor, an enthusiastic proponent of small-press publishing and a tireless community builder. For a writer whose work is routinely defined by its radical eclecticism, no texts in his formidable oeuvre more properly reflect the diverse, ephemeral and joyous elements of his practice than his trilogy: *love: a book of remembrances* (1974), *zygal: a book of mysteries and translations* (1985) and *art facts: a book of contexts* (1990). Out of print and hard to locate, these three works contain some of Nichol's best and most adventurous writing.

Publication dates for the trilogy are misleading. The poems contained in *love* were written between the fall of 1970 and the spring of 1971, while the lion's share of poems appearing in *zygal* were composed over the course of the following year from 1972 to 1973.[1] Economic setbacks postponed its publication by twelve years, leading its editors to pronounce (with a degree of humour): 'we promised it to the author in 1973. We promised it to you in 1974 and again in 1980. Now, at last, the world is ready ... '[2] Nichol's notebooks and letters confirm that he had completed a draft of *art facts* as early as October 1975, declaring it 'a gathering of survivors – stuff that's withstood the test of time – a companion piece to *zygal*.'[3] A letter to Richard Grossinger, editor of North Atlantic Books, shows that Nichol had attempted to publish it the following year in the spring of 1976, but it too met with financial obstacles, such that fourteen years would elapse before its eventual publication. Unlike the first two volumes, a number of the poems included in *art facts* date to the mid-1960s, while others originally slated for inclusion were replaced by texts written over the next decade. Nevertheless, all three books were conceived and largely written during the first half of the 1970s, during a period of overwhelming productivity.

Nichol's work during the 1960s had followed two distinct paths. At least this is how it looked in print: a lyric mode first anthologized in Raymond Souster's *New Wave Canada: The New Explosion in Canadian Poetry* (1966), which earned Nichol early praise among Canada's literary elite, and the minimalist 'typewriter concrete' collected in *Konfessions of an Elizabethan Fan Dancer* (1967), which aligned Nichol with an international consortium of avant-garde writers at home and abroad. His work would appear in Stephen Bann's *Concrete Poetry: Britain, Canada, United States* (1966), Emmett Williams's *An Anthology of Concrete Poetry* (1967) and Mary Ellen Solt's *Concrete Poetry: A World View* (1970). By the late 1960s, however, any generic division in Nichol's body of work (if ever there was one) would quickly disappear. *bp* (1967), for instance, consists of an artfully decorated box containing the short lyric volume *Journeying & the Returns*, a collection of loose-leaf visual poems called *Letters Home*, a record titled *Borders* and a flip book called *Wild Thing* (1967).

Over the half-decade preceding the publication of *love* (1974) – when the bulk of poems in the trilogy were written – Nichol would see to press *Two Novels* (1969), *Beach Head* (1970), *The True Eventual History of Billy the Kid* (1970), *Still Water* (1970), *ABC: The Aleph Beth Book* (1971), *The Captain Poetry Poems* (1971), *Monotones* (1971), *The Other Side of the Room* (1971), Books I and II of *The Martyrology* (1972), *Milt the Morph in Colour* (with Barbara Caruso, 1972) and *aleph unit* (1973). To this sizeable output now add Nichol's activities as editor of *The Cosmic Chef* (1970) and *grOnk* magazine, his live performances and recordings with the Four Horsemen and the tandem explorations with Steve McCaffery as the Toronto Research Group. The result is one of the most impressive outbursts of literary production by an author writing during the second half of the twentieth century.

Despite the lag between the publication of *love* and its sequels, Nichol's notebooks and correspondence with friends reveal a precise plan for the series. A letter addressed to *art facts* editor Charles Alexander records: 'the Basho translation pieces continue the Catullus impulse in *ZYGAL* and the "Ghosts" piece in *LOVE*. Other texts (like PRAYER etc.) are part of the same notion, of continuing certain threads thru this whole series while still allowing each book to stand on its own.' Moreover, 'each volume should come out from a different publisher' and should 'cover a fairly wide formal range (another characteristic of the series).'[4] The books 'thread thru' one another indeed, linked by conceptual strains and intertextual echoes. To be sure, *love*'s four separate segments – *ghosts, frames, love poems* and *allegories* – afford a tidier structure than *zygal* and *art facts*'s plaited design. The latter two books introduce celebrated sequences like *probable systems, The Actual Life of Language* and *dreamed anthology*. Nichol's process involved increasingly more labyrinthine and open-ended poetic structures, reflecting what the author calls 'the half-life of the poem.'[5]

By 1976, Nichol was already reflecting on *love*'s significance for his development as a writer. In it one finds 'my two obsessions,' he remarks: 'the eye – the page as a visual field – and the ear ... [brought] together.' *love* also develops several techniques with the comic strip, the breathline poem and the hand-drawn visual text that toy with their narrative logic as forms and their status as material texts. In 'Frame 4,' for instance, Nichol depicts an empty comic panel with the word 'outside' beyond its border. We are told in 'Frame 7': a 'frame runs around this phrase.' No panel surrounds these words, but of course Nichol's point is that there are always frames that shape our experience and inform our knowledge. Without the comic panel, is the frame now the book, the reader's experience, the nation, the world? Elsewhere in the volume, words replace drawings, such that signifiers are given licence to float freely: 'there is a sun setting / here there is a horizon / someone thinks' ('Frame 6'). These poems resemble certain Fluxus events and conceptual works that emphasize play and process, conflate art with life and, above all, require the reader's imaginative participation.

In *allegories* each poem-drawing compresses story into a single cluster of images, 'thus no linearity to the narrative but rather a grouping which the "reader" must "read" into a linear sequence.'[6] 'Allegory #22,' for instance, depicts the evolution of the letter L. Beginning as a horizontal bar, each successive drawing reveals a slightly taller stem reaching toward its cap height. A thought balloon hovers above its adolescent stage of growth, inside of which a capital letter L appears (an 'l' dreaming of growing up). Nichol's drawing tells the story of language's origin, not from phrase or word as the primordial unit of meaning, but from the typographic anatomy of letters – stems, bars, serifs, bowls – that constitutes the material building blocks in the life of language.

He recounts in a letter to Mary Ellen Solt that sometime in the spring of 1971 he realized he could incorporate his experiments with the comic form into the 'breath-line' poem. Evoking Olson's familiar term, if the poem was a field of forces within which a multiplicity of elements interact, then the letter, 'just like anything else[,] ... was an element in the poem.'[7] Olson keeps letters tethered to words. Nichol permits them to stand alone, performing rhythmic and expressive functions:

a mood of g
a presence of m

l k
r s y t n ('Trans-Continental')

In conversation with Caroline Bayard and Jack David, he explains how he began to think about words semantically, as if they were sentences that reveal hidden 'symbologies' in their letters (a technique providing the ground plan for the more formally adventurous passages in Books III and IV of *The Martyrology*). The word 'word' thus becomes 'w or d'; 'time' declares 't i'm e'; archaism warns 'arch a is m.' The alphabet becomes a shifting, dreamy landscape of permutable recreation. *love poems* is precisely that, an address to a lover, but the object of desire is none other than language itself. The poems in *love* 'expressed my feelings about the alphabet,' writes Nichol, 'celebrated my wedding to it.'[8]

The techniques developed in *love* persist throughout *zygal* and *art facts*, although Nichol abandons its discrete chapters. Instead, the second and third volumes adopt a structure of interlaced and open-ended sequences, creating a literary bazaar of imitations, translations, appropriations, performance pieces and quasi-scientific reports. We find poems 'for and after' Dante, bill bissett, George Bowering, Daphne Marlatt and others. *dreamed anthology* catalogues poems composed by friends that come to him in sleep. His task? Record them meticulously. In conversation with collaborator Steve McCaffery, Nichol describes his Basho and Catullus translations as 'conversations with the dead' – the Basho sequence evolving from a mini-tradition among several of his contemporaries engaged in creative misprision (McCaffery, Dom Sylvester Houédard, Dick Higgins, et al.).[9] And like the Dadaists, Situationists and Fluxus artists, Nichol's appropriation work draws heavily from newspaper headlines and advertisements, which he détourns in *The Actual Life of Language* sequence and 'deathad death'shead.' Just as he had intimated with the frottagic rubbings in *ghosts*, the trace of other writers appears inseparably linked to his own practice. In another example of breath-line letter play, Nichol's Duncan-inspired 'Poem Beginning with an Old Poem' makes this point with characteristic wit:

addition

    i
add
  it on

A final example: the wonderfully idiosyncratic *probable systems* applies parodic forms of quantitative analysis to reading, writing and the material book. 'ps 19' proposes a mathematical formula for measuring the reader's receptiveness to avant-garde texts; 'ps 17' offers an algebraic equation to determine the 'circumference of words'; 'ps 8' applies numerical values to letters in order to gauge the relative quantity of prose to poetry in a given text (thus resolving the prose poem dispute!); others visualize the movement of sentences, weigh speech and track the speed of thought. Nichol and McCaffery co-edited a special issue of *Open Letter* dedicated to 'Canadian ''Pataphysics,' a variant of Alfred Jarry's 'pataphysical 'science of imaginary solutions.' The subtle shift from elision to quotation signals both its departure 'into-beside-beyond' its site of origin and its function as a science of 'perpetually open citing.'[10] In their introduction, they offer Nichol's *probable systems* as the consummate exemplar of such writing.

Nichol remarks that his work from the early 1970s was written from 'a research point of view ... I've published things because that's the point I've reached and maybe somebody else can pick up on it. As opposed to the finished polished artifact.'[11] This last claim, emphasizing process over product, is dutifully recited by an untold number of poets writing during the later part of the twentieth century, but for Nichol the notion is inexorably linked to community-building. His TRG reports, co-authored with McCaffery, insist that research 'is symbiotic' and 'can function to discover new uses for potentially outdated forms and techniques.'[12] Nichol eschews notions of pure novelty and individual genius, opting instead for a poetic process understood as a laboratory of shared techniques and experiments. The TRG reports, the Four Horsemen workshops, the Institute of Creative Misunderstanding (Dick Higgins's term), the Eternal Network (Brecht and Filliou's term), the Institute for Alphabet Archaeology (Nichol's term) – these were playfully conceived places and spaces both tactile/local and discursive/international, established in collaboration via readings, festivals and correspondence with a group of likeminded poets and artists.[13] The poet is not an isolated figure. S/he is one who conducts an experiment with language, producing materials, methods and texts for a community of others who are free to transform and adapt them.

The acknowledgment pages in *zygal* and *art facts* make mention of plans for two more volumes: the elusive *ox, house, camel, door: a book of higher glyphs* and *truth: a book of fictions*. His unpublished papers show that he was writing both manuscripts simultaneously just before his death, but that each one was still very much in an early stage. Two notebook entries, both dated August 30, 1988 (approximately a month before he died), outline a rough list of possible inclusions for each.[14] Mercury Press later published a book called *truth* under the editorial direction of Irene Niechoda. The archival records kept at Simon Fraser University indicate that this text absorbed nearly the entire manuscript of *ox*, along with miscellany culled from Nichol's notebooks. Presumably this decision was made to meet the length criteria for book publication, since neither the drafts of *ox* nor *truth* were sufficient on their own. Instead of combining the manuscripts, one might have preserved the division between *ox*, *truth* and related miscellany by taking one's cue from Nichol's notebooks and drafts. Still, Mercury's edition brought to light a valuable collection of unpublished materials, including the wonderfully playful 'Catalogue of the "Pataphysical Hardware Company,' 'Studies in the Book Machine' and previously unpublished *probable systems*. It remains in print and hence does not form part of this collection.

It would seem that if Nichol had not encountered publishing obstacles, his trio would have likely been a quintet running parallel to *The Martyrology*. Of course, most readers would not have known that he was planning an ongoing series until the mid-1980s when *zygal* eventually appeared and *art facts* was announced in the former volume's back matter. How might this have changed the critical reception of Nichol's work? One can only speculate. His long poem has undoubtedly enjoyed a central position in the scholarly record, leading recent critics to challenge its hagiographic status at the expense of his more innovative work.[15] Like the thoughtfully edited *The Alphabet Game: A bpNichol Reader* (2007), *a book of variations* seeks to expand access to the extraordinary array of talents he developed in the trilogy, while placing it within a milieu of experiments in collaboration, plotless prose and translation techniques.[16]

In fact, many of the poems contained in *love – zygal – art facts* appear elsewhere, as illustrated broadsides, as chapbooks, and in small magazines. By the time Nichol was working on *love*, Ganglia Press had run its course and *grOnk* had taken its place as a more informal and inexpensive publishing endeavour. He recounts that subscriptions were done away with and the magazine distributed freely to an international mailing list.[17] In part, the DIY manner in which *grOnk* operated afforded its editor greater opportunity to use a range of formats: perfect-bound books, mimeographed card stock, stapled and looseleaf paper, and 3D objects. Nichol routinely experimented with typeface, ink colour, page dimensions and the ways in which texts were distributed. A poem such as 'Blues,' for instance, appears with and without title, as a limited-edition print, typescript in *Konfessions*, and typeset in most anthologies, all before gracing the cover of *love* in a bicolour typeface – a single instance of the word 'love' set in green. The poem is thus a variable object, capable of remediation and change.

Nichol famously calls this variation 'borderblur,' a term he defines as 'poetry which arises from the interface, from the point between things.'[18] Yet this concept pertains to more than just genre. Borderblur subtends the traditional boundaries of material book design in its numerous contexts and conditions. Even the category of the Author is not safe from contamination. Nichol's collaborations with visual artists, The Four Horsemen, the TRG and an international group of concrete poets produced innumerable conceptual models and aesthetic techniques that these writers understood were the shared ideas of a poetic commons. Borderblur is thus more expansive and subtle than the now canonical terms found in our dictionaries of postmodern culture ('multi-modal,' 'inter-disciplinary,' etc.). It denotes a practice that unsettles the conceptual divisions of genre, disturbs the book as a unified artifact and disperses the exalted status of the author.

George Bowering would jest in conversation with the author: 'the next thing I expect is to see a bpNichol room where people can lean against the walls and (LAUGHTER) take escalators.'[19] An unexpected truth resonates with this proposition. The prolific output in Nichol's trilogy, read in all its signature variation, becomes an imaginative structure wherein to conduct an experiment of your own, a space in which to run around and get lost, or even start a sultry love affair with a letter or two.

Note on the text

Nichol lamented that books had become rarified, 'holy' objects. But rather than abandon the format altogether, he wanted books to rejoin the ranks of 'postcards' and 'posters,' insisting that they should retain 'the qualities of a precious object – well-crafted, etc. – but [remain] cheaply available to anyone who wanted to own one.' We chose a single-volume format over a three-volume set in order to reduce cost for readers. This decision breaks one of Nichol's cardinal rules: that each volume should appear with a different publisher, a feat too logistically demanding to realize. That said, we wish to recognize Talonbooks and Chax Press, the original publishers of *love* and *art facts* respectively. Along with Ellie Nichol, these partners exhibit the kind of open source community, camaraderie and friendship that bpNichol actively fostered.

Taking our cue from Nichol's own practice, we attempt in this collection to emphasize his commitment to the material text while recognizing the merit of remediation. The dimensions of *love* (6" by 9") are slightly larger than *zygal* and *art facts* (5¾" by 8¾"); *a book of variations* (5½" by 8¾") finds a place in between. Visual poems appear at 95 percent of their published size and maintain a comparable image-to-margin ratio. Type is set in Goluska and Classic Grotesque.

Notes

1 Nichol, 'A Letter to Mary Ellen Solt,' 1973, *Brick: A Journal of Reviews* 23 (Winter 1985): 18–19. 19.

2 *zygal*, back cover.

3 Nichol, 'English Book,' Notebooks, MsC 12 d. 13; letter to Richard Grossinger, 8 Apr. 1976, MsC 12 d. 1–12, bpNichol Papers, Contemporary Literature Collection, Special Collections and Rare Books, Simon Fraser University.

4 Letter to Charles Alexander, 30 Aug. 1988, MsC 12 d. 15, 'Art Facts' folder, bpNichol Papers, Contemporary Literature Collection, Special Collections and Rare Books, Simon Fraser University.

5 Geoff Hancock, 'The Form of the Thing: An Interview with bpNichol on Ganglia and *grOnk*,' 1986, *Rampike* 12.1 (Winter 2000–2001): 30–36. 35.

6 Nichol, 'A Letter to Mary Ellen Solt,' 18–19.

7 Caroline Bayard and Jack David, 'Interview with bpNichol,' *Out-Posts* (Erin: Press Porcépic, 1978), 16–40. 38–39.

8 Nichol, 'A Letter to Mary Ellen Solt,' 19.

9 Nichol, 'The Annotated, Anecdoted, Beginnings of a Critical Checklist of the Published Works of Steve McCaffery,' *Open Letter* 6.9 (Fall 1987): 67–92. 75.

10 TRG, 'Introduction to Canadian ''Pataphysics,' *Open Letter* 4.6/7 (Winter 1980–1981). Reproduced in *Rational Geomancy: The Kids of the Book Machine, The Collected Research Reports of the Toronto Research Group, 1973–1982* (Vancouver: Talonbooks, 1992): 301–303. 301.

11 Bayard and David, 'Interview with bpNichol,' *Out-Posts*, 28.

12 TRG, 'Manifesto,' *Open Letter* 2.4 (Spring 1973): 75. Reproduced in *Rational Geomancy*, 23.

13 For sources of these terms and their uses, see Nichol and McCaffery, *Rational Geomancy*; The Four Horsemen, *Prose Tattoo: Selected Performance Scores* (Milwaukee: Membrane Press, 1983); Dick Higgins, 'The Mail-Interview with Dick Higgins,' By Ruud Janssen, Fluxus Heidelberg Center, 1995, web; George Brecht and Robert Filliou, 'The Eternal Network,' *Teaching and Learning as Performing Arts* (Koeln: Koening, 1970), 197–207; Nichol, 'Probable Systems 22a/TTA 25,' *art facts: a book of contexts* (Tucson: Chax Press, 1990), 111–112.

14 Nichol's notebook entry records the following:

're OX, HOUSE, CAMEL, DOOR / Aug 30th, 1988: Various alphabet poems "a bee see [?] elfy" etc. / selection from 26 ALPHABET / 3-D H; [?] on the 26 letters / H AT MIDNIGHT, SYMPHONY, etc. / dream H series / PURGE ME WITH H[.]

re TRUTH: A Book of Fictions / Aug 30th, 1988 / Find SKETCHING 3 (in one of [?] red York booklets) / find NEGATIVES 4 + find NEGATIVES 3 / check on PS30 in origin [?] i.e. Masculin/Feminin to [?] thing in HIRI / redo PS32 / what about the pataphysics catalogue idea? / include the uncollected non-series short fictions[.]'

From 'The Vel (-lour/-vet/-lum) Notebook,' MsC 12 d. 13, bpNichol Papers, Contemporary Literature Collection, Special Collections and Rare Books, Simon Fraser University.

15 See, for example, Frank Davey, 'Exegesis / Eggs à Jesus: *The Martyrology* as a Text in Crisis,' *Tracing the Paths: Reading ≠ Writing 'The Martyrology*,' ed. Roy Miki (Vancouver: Line/Talonbooks, 1988), 38–51. Also, Davey, 'bpNichol + 10: Some Institutional Issues Associated with the Continued Reading of Texts Known as "bpNichol,"' 5–13, Darren Wershler-Henry, 'Argument for a Secular Martyrology,' 37–47, and Christian Bök, 'Nickel Linoleum,' 62–74, bpNichol + 10, *Open Letter* 10.4 (Fall 1998).

16 The recent reissue of *Konfessions*, ed. Nelson Ball (Toronto: Coach House, 2004), *The Captain Poetry Poems*, ed. Jay Millar (Toronto: Book Thug, 2011), *Organ Music* (Windsor: Black Moss, 2012), and the publication of *The Alphabet Game: A bpNichol Reader*, eds. Lori Emerson and Darren Wershler-Henry (Toronto: Coach House, 2007) has thankfully made a much wider range of work more accessible.

17 In the same document, Nichol explains that *grOnk* had two focused objectives: 'to argue for (a) a visually oriented poetry in general & (b) Canadian visual poetry in the context of the world-wide movement in particular.' See 'GANGLIA PRESS/grOnk,' MsC 12 d. 15, bpNichol Papers, Contemporary Literature Collection, Special Collections and Rare Books, Simon Fraser University.

18 Nicette Jukelevics, 'Interview with b. p. Nichol,' 1974, in 'A Bibliography of Canadian Concrete, Visual and Sound Poetry 1965-1972,' MA thesis, Concordia University, 1975. Reproduced in *Meanwhile: The Critical Writings of bpNichol*, ed. Roy Miki (Vancouver: Talonbooks, 2002): 133–139. 134.

19 George Bowering, 'Cutting Them All Up: An Interview with BP Nichol,' *ALPHABET* 18/19 (1971): 18–21. 18.

20 Nichol, 'Primary Days: Housed with the Coach at the Press, 1965 to 1987,' *Provincial Essays* 4 (1987): 19–25. Reproduced in *Meanwhile*, 422–429. 426, 428.

love
a book of remembrances

for margaret avison & earle birney

'Where one or two have won:
(The silver reaches of the estuary).'

ghosts

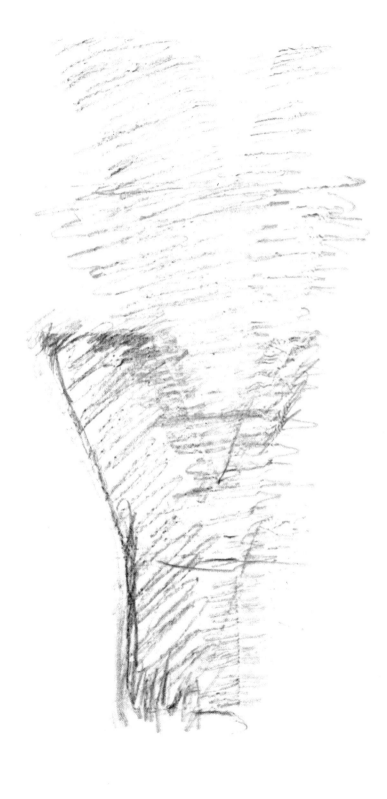

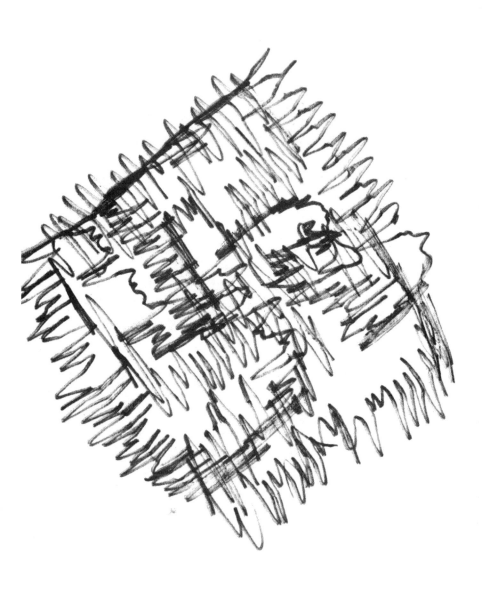

frames

Frame 1

Frame 2

sky

something which watches quietly

earth

Frame 3

outside

Frame 4

a bird flies

a face emerges

Frame 5

there is a sun setting

here there is a horizon

someone thinks

Frame 6

a frame runs around this phrase

Frame 7

this frame is empty

Frame 8

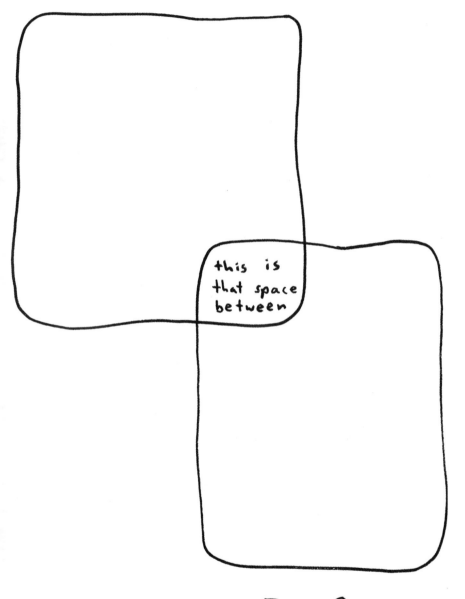

this is
that space
between

Frame 9 + 12

here there be birds

sun

perhaps a moon (it is white)

blue sky

mountains

a letter lies on its side

Frame 10

Frame 11

Frame 13

there is no relationship

a hand waves

Frame 14

a bird has fallen thru. it
is injured. the sky is blue. soon
a face will emerge + smile.

Frame 15

clouds

a bird

mountains

a river

something is moving

Frame 16

love poems

stills

1

a cloud

h

probably nothing happens

2

a man in front of a mirror
an h in front of an m

everything is on its side

something whistles

3 *for steve mcCaffery*

o

h

later an e appears

4

here there is a w

if i wait long enough it floats away

5

u
e w r
l
m n o p
q

6

r r r
e
s l p t u
no

7

how high is a question

up

d u c l m
v t

8

elbow

the room is still

window
w q

9

l
l l l
l l
   l

10

moon

cloud window green

up
up up

t

11

a
a
a

12

the sun or a circle

o
b

maybe a cloud floats thru

13 *one more for steve mcCaffery*

e e e e
e e e e
e e e e
f

14

sun

moon

h

h

15

a longer line intersects

green

something coloured red

where an h should be there is an m instead

16

o o o

later a line appears

p? d? q? b?

feb 20/71

clover

1

h h h
m

l p r s t
u

    v w i
r b l t
c q
    c q

r
r
rrrr
u

another u

if i am i i am
if i is i i is

blue
blue
blue

neither is each other

if green is red there is white
if blue is yellow there is green

h

now i is m
something which is useless floats away

mmmmmmm
mmmmmmm

i being black there is white
w or q
perhaps an l or a z

here someone pauses to breathe
e is taken a breath
th

    b
bbb b
bbb
     d
q
  l m n
p s j v
q
   q
q

a line lingers
something which is not
a letter in the middle of a sky
neither grey nor blue

white
white
white

white
white
white

white
white
white

i

t

a b or
a b or

white
white white white
white   white

a line which is someone
a circle that becomes
a colour that doesn't fit

e or f

l m n
l m n

o

o

o

o

a sky

an h

a line that intersects

a circle

black
black
black
black

blue

a green that becomes

a red

a yellow that lingers

an h or
a p
          maybe an m again
an n or
a field that is green
a sky that is blue
an h that is broken

ooooooooooooooo

w w
w w
t u v
w
w

2

s
s s
v

t u l m
p p t r p
s

   s a
s b s a a
a a a
s m n o a a
s s
sssssssss

b j k r t u v a d l
p m n o l s r w p t
o v w
e
e

g q l k k k
k t s r p

n
   m
n m n n n
m m m
o p l m n o opens
x is a line
u
   i is cut
the a discarded
t

p l s x v

z z z z

3

c m n o able
sky
        a white that is white
t t t
u l o r b
green s o
blue but able
able to be able
b c d e
f i r a l m x

a b a b
be able to be
c or w or
unable to be a
be b be h be
a or v or
blue green white
green green blue white
white blue white blue
green green green green

next to o
a t or e
d f the cloud the
w or sky or
m r f h i j

l o l o l m n o
the w suspended
the l removed
everything becomes itself

d t s r t
j l v q m n a f
s h c i z t z k g

maybe an o
itself four times
green green green green
unable to be o
be c be d be
h i s l q r k
be l be x be

no

the sky

the h or the m

e belonging to another
f
  f

clouds

a green sky

blue being blue
there is h or m or
i

an h that is h
an i that is i
something which is neither

y

w or q

l

m n o
t s b d l m
n o
t

d b t
c r   r

a blank spot

something which is not

d

l p t q
r s v
m n o l k

a man is running

c

an empty sky

a bird

q

a strange moon

a different sun

light q l white
the able blue d m
o b c r whispering

white

blue white

blue
        green red blue
yellow white white green
c d c d
n n

o

the sun

o

the cloud

o

the bird

o

the man

h

h h

h

heaven & hell

1

h h white h h
the h the the the
heaven height where the
h h h

hard when oh help
h h h h h
heat heaven hard
h the
when when when

2

white hold three eight
sleigh shingle thumb
thunder whine white theme
shunt
       shunt

3

whether

4

simply ever backwards
an opening
                gone

g

i

noting

5

halleleujah
halleleujah

halleleujah

halleleujah

this then this
then this that the other

halleleujah
halleleujah

thin

whistling

against explanation

oh the a be
an or and and
c

c d q o p
stops

whistle up gorge leg
laughter m l steep
la lune la lune

low l t s z
v v o b q r
la tigre i y w

moon

june

spoon

a small song that is his

adore adore
adore adore
an opening an o
an h a leg a table or
a window & a w
a sky that is d
a lake that is f
e

d e f
f f f f
d d
    e e e
d f f e f e
f e f e

me
you or me or
i h & d
m e
e f d
o

d f h e w

f

f e w h d

o

w d

f

thrush throat grief – why?

1

mine in sticks
crisis
          six piping sing

suspension

certain tensions
telescoping

something which is hidden

hi!

2

everyone enters something
everything becomes then

end

begin

each one
three

5 7 8
9 10

3

absolutely

always

you
younger yet

hey!

       (maybe)

4

oh

today opens
tomorrow closes

swoon

top older troop
overt folding fold
dock

obviously old
overtly young

oblivious mother port
possible women
bold pole polite sloop

shone shone

5

up under thumb punch
you supper lucky cup
muddle

muddle puddle thru
blue cut hump pun
nun nouveau true

out

louvered run touch pup mud
stun stumble stump
crumble

       out

           out

6

paid average
awfully glad at that

any way at all
anyway and maybe
awful awful awful

yass yass!!

perhaps

(later a dream
a statement

meant as lately
later late

                        March 9/71

music

do

mi

d o m i do mi
la so l a s o d
ra fa mi so la ti
t i l a a f i r m
s o s o s

ti

do

trans-continental

1

an h moves past an m
an i becomes an r

someone throws a snowball

o p
t r s u
v v v

w

i i i i

2

x d

one mile

a sky which is grey
blue

do not serve yourself

l e
4 3 1 2 2

3

z

zero then nothing

3
6 9 10
13 5

here a z becomes an e
becomes an m a w

4

a d in a cloudbank
an r by a sea

perhaps it is a river
passes over

sky

sun

a town
in which the r becomes an l

5

a drainage ditch

an o

white white white
on a pole in a field
white white grey

two trees
three or four
est

ouest

est cinq est sept est
huit huit huit

6

this many miles from home
r becomes everything

s t t a p
z t m n n
o q l r
v s c d g

later there is hope
or lessness

perhaps you dream

t
v n h l p
z w a b

7

ness

ing

ch th sl le
e

a rocking motion
a creaking sound

an ack
a ly

8

crump cring
kasno alty

y

j a
t b

v t l m n q o p

b

b c d e g p
t v a j k l

l m n

m n o p

n o p a b
c d r f q

v
z
p

9

snow
s o o o
w n o s
n n n n

a white field
a green

      (dark

         darker than dark

        est

a blue that is grey
an e

climbs up thru the cloudy sky
overwhelms me

10

j

r

k t o v m
l s me

you or i

we

11

up & down

wavey

w w w
w w w w

m
n u u n
m m

p

the sky turns greyer
turns erer

white & black

dark green

a t crossed by an h

resembles nothing more than
resembling

inging

rrrrrr

12

37-3

an h that is beyond me
turns brown
turns around

h or h

i then t

pause

39

today the weather is not fine
yesterday it was worse

152
nothing to do but dream
d g m v

13

snow at the window

white room

blue blue blue
blue blue blue
blue blue bluer

dark green & white
straight with branches
bending

g or h or

grey white grey
white grey white

wind

a sun which is hidden
a t in a snowbank

h h
h h

an l that insists itself
insists itself
insists

14

hornpayne to armstrong
h to a

ha!

ah ah ah ah

t
u v m l k
r s p

stops

s to s

bless this

15

a lake in a snowstorm
m's in clumps

o's & h's pile together

maybe an occasional a
perhaps a t

a sentence occurs
ending with the pronoun me

16

there is too much white
too many h's

life holds too much s or m
t b j f
m t

t's pile up on t's
r's are scattered

an s lies broken in
the corner of
this room

17

a y by a road
a lake or a sea

wheat wheat wheat
brown among white

a fence
a fancy fold
a hill

i r k

a lady

light light light

18

a right a left
a flat latitude
fat laugh

a t h or e

here a longer line erupts suddenly

my toes are pointed west
my heels are pointed east

c

19

d b f g e
r z t l m
o o p d q b
l o c d k r n

y

t v z q p
l o r i k

b o m q l
l b c d y
j f
r t
m p h i i y t

20

empty eyes
empty skies
z z y

y x x w
w v v
u u t t s
s

bless this
i did say
yes yes yes
i did say i did say
bless this yes
bless this yes
bless yes yes

21

three deer
a field

a road that ends where h begins

two t's again

a w
a q
an ordinary o

later a z
a p

a field where horses pissed
yellow yellow

22

trees that are white not brown
with snow falling down

a footprint
an a

everything rises

a circle
a stadium
a town

a place where the road is brown not white

voices i cannot hear

h e l

wainwright

23

now there is a mountain
big not small
dark not light

soon there is a sun setting
a green tree
a memory of a time not now
h gone brown
falling to a c

d rises
r sets

the sooner the l
the later it gets

24

4
3 in a row
0 1 2

l t q r
farther than f
g

c d c d
l m n o
l m n o
p

repeated

not foreseen

dreams
in which the dreamer dreams a dreamer
dreams a dreamer
dreams a dreamer
dreaming

25

m m m
an n which slants
disappears in o

u w u
m m m n
u v
o

grey sky
i wonder why

tear blue like you

c o k
j r
   j u

26

if there is lack of light is there no light

lack is black
height is white

why is h always h

now it is i
now t

z y x b
r v m n l

hello

yesterday i had a dream

last night i slept with the blind up

u t m d
l l
l

27

o dreaming
l sets

r rises black
blue blue blue

even the white turns green
purple
            black

black black black
back to blue

e rises

no

e does not rise
it is a dream

somewhere on this train
ryme schemes

28

g in a station
going white

wheat in a pool
number 8

7

a line that doesn't fit

6 in a row

g

29

more music
less o

balance

a pair of opposites that don't attract

t

a height of m
a weight of b
of a &

do i know you?
no!

a z or a p or an f

30

just another just another

broken heart
half-hearted dream

just another h another h another t

31

ing
inger

ongoing
undone

a voice that is soft is h or r

accent

a book that is full is empty

l z j q
g f g

    (unfinished

    another voice

    m s
    a b d

    no choice of z)

32

e's in a cloud
voices that distract
e or e or e

f g a d l m k
r s o b j i

a distant v
a hum

a lady who is glum is sad

things ain't so bad

r

n or p

33

eyes in the dark
red not white

a starting point that is not right

an observation in a train station
a standing around

an h left lying on the ground

34

m
m z t p q
l y r k k k
j a h i w

o p d a
l b m z i
h r j r

is that right?
yes it fits

a narrow i
a thin t
an n that disappears

an m
an l
a g

35

a fantasy that fails to erupt
a disappointment

a sad pup
a happy kitten

two children asleep in the same bunk

an h by an m
an i by a t

here there is a vision

a choir sings

alleleuia
alleleuia
alleleuia

36

a longing for flesh
a flash of long

a lingering look
a languid mood

an l in a pool of pepsi

a cola
an a

(thinks)

something stops
something begins

rocking
l to m
nothing in between

is z is v is q is d

z to a

l d h z q t j

37

dark where there should be light

hot pants
cold thots

an r ringed in mist
later an s
then a t

if only the moon came up
the l would rise

settles on my shoulders

mood

38

a trance state
a continental trance

je ne sais pas monsieur
je ne sais pas madame

hello in the morning
goodbye in the afternoon

it has been h or w knowing you
y or m

it has been z
t u v l k
j r j

39

a face above a mountain
an m above a c

l j r u p k
m s z y v b d

i already said that

it is a snow cloud
an f day
a q g r

a fish in a river too cold to swim in

an absence of crowds

40

a saint
a gesture in the sky

an m on a mountaintop
a sequence of o's

a catalogue
a heaven
a vision of vision

h i r m
s t
l q

41

a new beginning
an ending

a slowing down
a speeding up

an arc in a park
an f in a rainstorm

2's or 3's
4 5 7

a leaning back
a falling forward

tree stumps

42

a needle
a fir
an e

l y j k m n
o z w u
v t m n n
k s l

sing ing

a bell on a breast
a blessed beast
bust

j or h
k or m

43

hair that is blonde is long

a dirty hand

a land that is lost
forgotten

a little girl that's frightened

a mood of g
a presence of m

l k
r s y t n

44

an ending a beginning
a beginning to see an end

a line that extends then collapses

a lax breath
he lacks it

a tree by a track
a rack & a scream

a tension
a lack of it
a lick

a lucky strike
a struck lock

an a that can't pretend

45

is this the end
it is not the end
we will say it is the end

a g k or l
m t z y v
w w
u u
l k r p p
d o k j r

the sun is up
the sky is blue

look at the grey clouds

i see them

y y y y
y y y

46

a b c d
f g e i
j j j j j
k l m
k l m
n o
    p

a c o or n
q v z w p
t t y a
b x u

47

green & red
black among white

a lighter sky
a darker hill

a u or z

narrow

thin but long

t p j l

48

a sand bar
an old car

a chocolate
a noise

t p l m n
o o o

a road by a track
a toad on a back 40

3 or 2
one e f

bridge

truck

sky eye

49

final finale
definite end end

h w w t
hope now awful hat

here
h e r e

heir & hair
or hare air

weir

wierdly y & d
j k k
g t

toronto–vancouver
march 13–16 1971

glady's poem

up is down
as down is up

a cradle & a rug in a rain storm

a g & an f
an r of seeing you
being with you
m & p

hot tumble heart pin
just best can't chin show
loving & knowing
stumble

speech is speech is speech

a pumpkin &
a tunnel a
tornado

march 22/71
12:45 a.m.
vancouver

formless faces

1

blue

gut turn red green
scree crag face fold
tumbledown
2

the simplest things hold nothing
holds the simplest things

an empty window behind a tree

ringing

2

if you hold up your hand
you hold up your hand

is that high enough?

no

there is no use to
a question mark my words i say
words & words & words

**an interlude in which saint ranglehold addresses
anyone who'll listen**

1

a light in a tree
a hand in a crowd
memory

whistle

now we will change directions
this time for good

what is the structure of heaven
it is a circle within a circle ad nauseam

if i am to stop & talk to you you must give me reason
i am a busy man

h z y k
l r p t m
u u

2

what is the meaning of meaning

it is whistling when the thunder claps or pissing when
     it rains

did you get the groceries

i tried but they were closed

when i asked a man to consider theory he said
i will think on it when i have a spare moment

3

despair is an air you sing

sorrow is to row your boat nowhere

h is not t
i is not m

whatever was is & will be again

poem beginning with lines from a dream

r n t
r n t
raggedy ann & andy

n e u
n e u
winnie the pooh

o k l e
o k l e
uncle wiggily

r s v p j
n l p q r a b
s t d n
s t u

lost angles

let us put this in focus
let us understand why

anger is as sudden as as

young dreams   older fears
the nearness of you
likely as not nearly new

mostly old catalogues
lists
liable to capsize

sudden

holden &
well
        yes
                collapse as

as likely nearly not new

something is old as nothing

nearly yearly the millennium come round again

fourths of a moment
airy pleasure
gone

to what gain
to whit
                none
known or un
the wise

threading send
or then
                hover
which is lover on
the rind the
pit of it

alpha beta
game as the next one
man i mean

oh i wish these lines were longer longer
the music you can hear
familiar river

almanac

a live is not alive
a corn is not

huit wheat (how sweet
ly done ly
ding)
       sing that song was sung
sang sun

fort

artery to heart to
ordinary ford
ing of
      the shallow part
& parcel &
'i am all tied up'
too busy to dream

i was happy there

he was happy

sea's son
i set sail or
he is gone away
gunned weight in heat
the sun
      sea's under the sea

interr relationships
lock up the heart

no knowing then that way

no

oh pen
            (clothes in disarray
crumpled

a phone call
all phony

fend off the end

it is over
so very over

symphony

allegories

Allegory #1

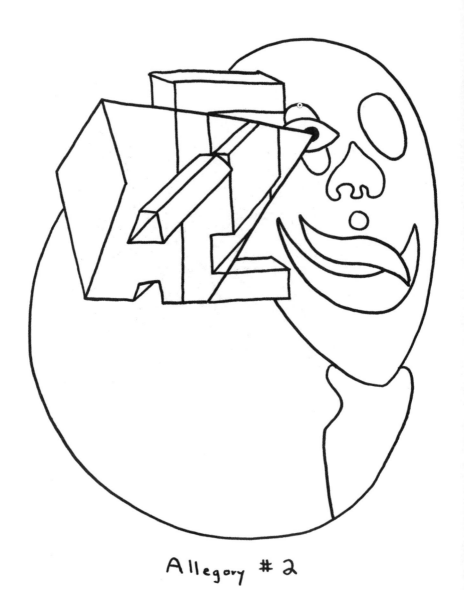

Allegory # 2

Allegory #3

Allegory # 4

Allegory #5

Allegory # 6

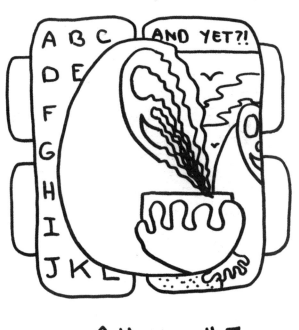

Allegory #7

Allegory # 8

Allegory #9

Allegory # 10
(for Steve McCaffery)

Allegory # 11

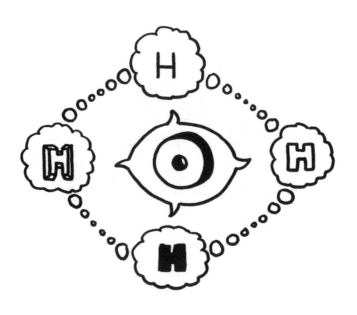

Allegory # 12

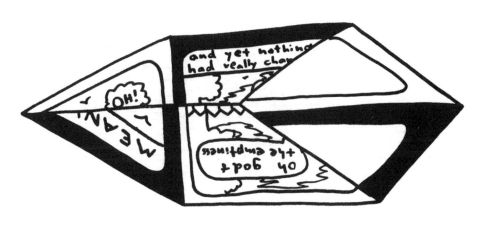

Allegory # 13

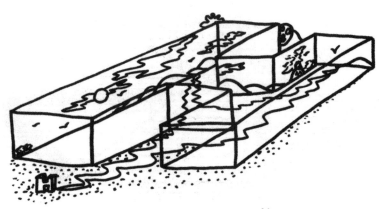

Allegory # 14

Allegory # 15

Allegory # 16

Allegory # 17

Allegory #18

Allegory # 19

Allegory #20

Allegory # 21

Allegory #22

Allegory # 23

Allegory #24

Allegory # 25

Allegory # 26

Allegory # 27

Allegory #28

Allegory #29

Allegory # 30

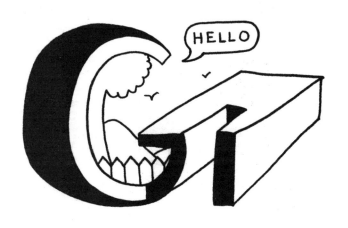

Allegory #31

Allegory # 32

zygal
a book of mysteries and translations

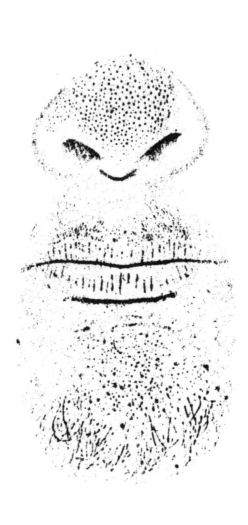

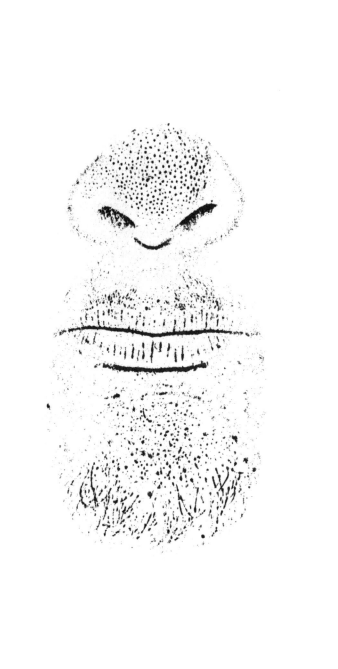

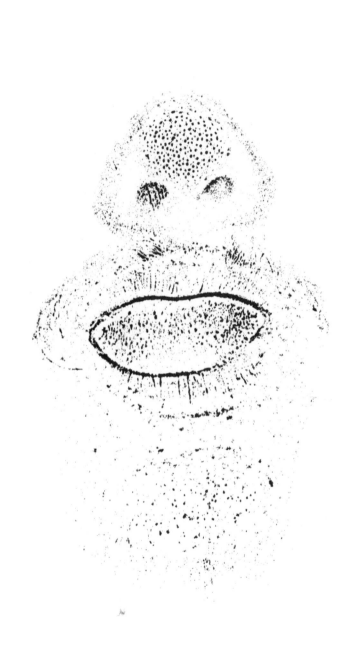

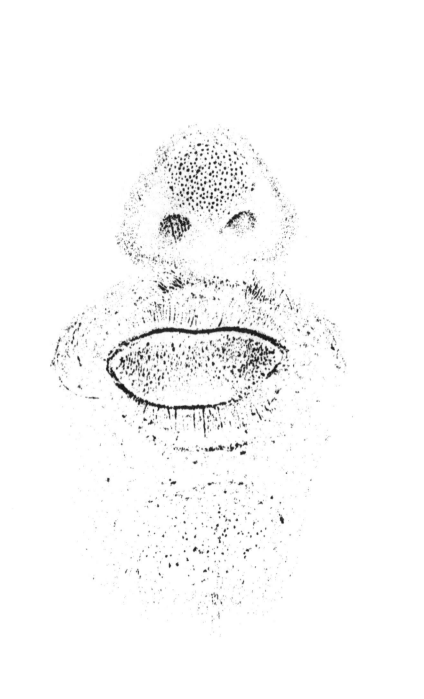

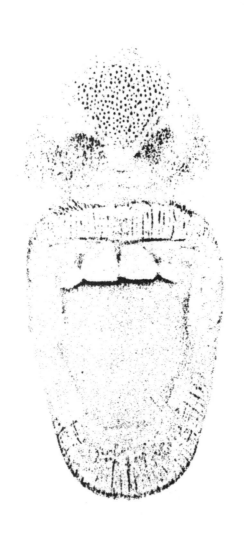

whatever the dream of numbers means
whatever the slumber that is never broken
the spoken word & the written
together end the spell

for paul rafael & steve

song for saint ein

i look at you this way

noun then verb

these are my words

i sing to you

•

no separation no

the same thing

i am these words
these words say so

somewhere i exist separate from this page
this cage of sounds & signs

i am this noise

my voice says so

Emblems

for james reaney

1

a or b

line of sky
    earth

here a tree is seen

               an eye
z or y

another bird

'the uncreating word'

a dreamed thot
'hand in hand'

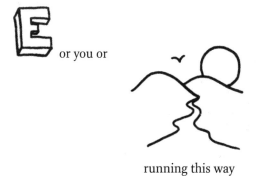

or you or

running this way

LAND e
SCAPES a

anyway
        you can

2

e l y or w

i am   you are   he is

this this or this

his t precedes me (my i)

time

      the cross comes before the essential split

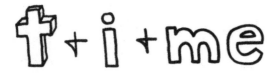

or it
     the metis
time juggled
followed by the s curve
gabriel dumont &
how he tried to serve
as best he could

forked tongue

the split

l.p.'s precede me

i stands before the cross
two things equated
how the record 'captures his sound'
thieves &
a crucifixion

the lady on the bus
talked to herself
answered her own questions

own as self

she is 'possessed'
is 'not in possession of

her faculties'
teach

the cross
followed by each
one of us

literal

a juggling of the real

a
disrupted by
its own suffering

illumination embodied in
acknowledging the real
weights & measures of
the language

3

rife

a rELief

lief to
re turn to you

the fife &
the leaf

he is marching
in time
            in
sea
    son

h

a hELi

copt or
gnostic
            nosegay

the e the l the
spanish way of saying
the particular

le el
fall
      fell

fill
      full

4

for sharon smith

a girl
kisses
a girl

a girl
a girl

the words twirl

two pairs of
lips

DUKE OF EARL EARL

four ears' l's

lobes

oboes & bells

5

a kiss is just this

this is his h
           or i
the motion
          music
sick/ly
      muse
          ocean swell

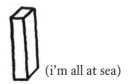 (i'm all at sea)

late   ly   ward   en   terse

'i want nothing to do with me'

denial &
its follow thru

THE DIVINE M

THE VISION

v is
the ion
          to end
conclusion

c on c
on LUSi

6

ennui

a stillness at
the heart of
the word

          n

at the heart of the alphabet

                         m &

w or d

always
that choice

ch or v

a b c d
w x y z

4 & 4

a probable system or

equidistant from either end and
reversed

that perfect balance the or is
forms the 'word'

7

heel to toe

i place one
right between the uprights

no one roars as the word soars

q r s t

i take the once-removed option

the measure is THAT much
the space between
the letters displacement
ENERGY

real to seal
the tomb door closes as
the letter
            clicks in place

it is
      the dead letter office
officer
          i am breaking into

alpha's bet
leaves the bookies broke

can you make it to the track

the sentence is the rent hence
the lung's wage paid
wasted on a fixed race
horses leave the post
mark
        time

mark or mask
the ark asked to save us
chases the dove across the wave
shits on us
hits home

i'd write you a letter

you're too far away

(the scene is later today   i'm reading this poem again rewriting it
    m then n   it makes more sense)

n to follow
the omnipresent A

8

the that
you hang your hat on

the lidded t

you blow your top

op art
        e
            rator
i'll see you later

such a feminine case

he frenched the letter la t
le t t
        er

lately
            arriving punctually
leaves you with the ly/ing
motion of
your hand's
connection with
the arc of
your spinning brim

(connect ion with the act the emblem becomes clear   my
head is right between my shoulders are too near together
                                                                    (the
late **R**   passes thru the room whistling   trans-continental
on a different track   waiting for willie's w to whisk us back)

that hat

that same same hat

9

when f is old
it folds over

when s is old
it's sold

twice told
the tale gets tangled
the odd story
of god & his gold

i am up in heaven heavin
heathen is a hen in heat

she wants her cock doc
C.O.D.

god on the barrelhead
she is barreled over
whelmed

the hands at the helm

the **⌐** and

at the **⌐**
elm's changed

                 the tarot unfolds

the hanged **G**
dangles by a golden chain

the moon rises
two circles in the alphabet's heart

l m n o
p
    the loop is
a reversal of the pool

G drowns

water is a noose he swallows
chokes him

when **G** is old
it turns cold

when H is old
it holds

       still

saint of illness

s till the hens come home

happy

Toronto–London–Vancouver
dec 24 1972–feb 7 1973

Sonnet Sequence

april 73

Probable Systems

thot probes for rob

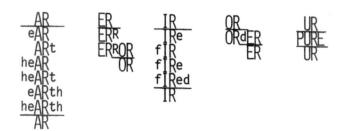

Untitled

sometimes as other sums of time are measured the day is not dark no
but bright the light the actual pleasure that the sun is upon your skin
you live inside your body   sometimes or this one time the line is
right to be spoken not as some time or other marked as the moving
point is disjointed ripped out of time but as is seen the scene set not
as set or play but moments reality continuums & not glum no seen
in this way   all times times could be as they are now   assuming
the form
          the 'tu' (familiar phrase)
          all days to be lived as pleasure
          inside the skin of history
          we know no measure of

          why poems are (for me)
          that highest form of reality
          i speak my mind   sing
          my song
          long as the ear can catch the tune
          the poem *is* the rune
          as the man the man
          how you hand it on
          one to the other
          part of the action of
          living
          giving
          what you can
            & i saw clearly as one does see the eye peels away (no
other way to describe it) that layer of feeling blinds the mind & i saw
clearly the poem is the man the man the rune & time the concept 'he
sings his tune as long as he can'

for the saints (their genre)

```
        A²
A  E
B  H³      D²
G  I  D²  H
I  N² E³  I  N  N  I  N  G
T³ O³ G
W⁵    R²
      S²
      T
```

early october poem

there is a well in this world in which our faces float
surface at the moment we appear
as if there were a dream we could return from
a mirror we could walk thru to ourselves

there is a path leads there thru a wood that i have travelled
often from an urge to be alone
a lady who is flesh & vaginal
i take for my own

there is a window in which a light appears
a door i knock upon
song sung
          a younger one who is also me
          i am afraid to know

sometimes at night i go there
gaze into my face as it appears
turn back into that lady's arms
no harm surely to befall me
watch myself thru the window playing
saying to myself 'is this what you are?
is this all?'

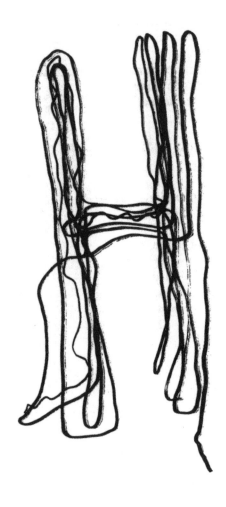

Self-contradiction

abcdefghijklmNO

from CATULLUS poem XXVII

Minister with pure oil Falerni
my calloused armour injuries,
and let Postumiae lube the magistrate,
his bride's seen his bridle sores.
at your hole you bet the stinker'd bite, he's limp,
wine's pernicious, and all love's semen
migrates: hiccups from his mouth onto your thighs.

three small songs for gladys hindmarch

language is or was or has been has been said before i did say
once as gertrude did commas are disgusting little things such
sucks she did did not say said they do things for you you should
do for yourself they make you lazy   ruling out commas what
did i say was it yesterday or the day before sitting on this plane
drunk there is this nun behind this guy is badgering says he
knows something about her he will tell her later but he knows
her   late or early sitting up i'm tired no well okay this one
time son sure you can stay up & listen to the radio   tomorrow
i'll step off to continue as words or language does that sense of
it continually run together in our heads articulate the causal
separations   when the baby comes the silver spoon screaming
from the mouth we are blessed   all that is best & wonderful

•

up is down
as down is up

a cradle & a rug in a rain storm

a g & an f
an r of seeing you
being with you
m & p

hot tumble heart pin
just best can't chin show
loving & knowing
stumble

speech is speech is speech

a pumpkin &
a tunnel a
tornado

•

images imagine packages this is the way it is   yesterday the
wind blew today the sky is blue   if the wind blows does the
sky blow

this is a story i mentioned before imagine the imagination can
you   this is how you begin   the image is imagination
    dear gladys   today the sky is without form it is colour only
or imagine how the sky's form is imaginary (it is) as saint ory
told me that was a different story i could not imagine then

scene: a small window completely filled with blue   the action
    is from left to right   imagine someone walks thru   a
    saint addresses you

                this is the way i sing my song   this is the way
you write the tune   imagine imagining imagining can you

probable systems 3

unresolved 9/10/71 4:37 a.m.

```
chief
   i f
 l ief
bel ief
belch
      (b − 2
       c − 2
       e − 2 + 3 = 5
       f − 4
       h − 2          five
       i − 4          fi ef
       l − 3          ive
                   (e − 3
                    f − 3 + 1 = 4
                    i − 3
                    v − 2)        four
                                  our
                                  ou — (french)


                                  ou
                                  or
                                  ou
                                     (o − 3
                                      2u + lr = ?
```

error noted
4:54 a.m.

in second transformation the total of 2f + 1f was mistakenly added
to the right hand f to give f − 3 + 1 = 4   this should read
2 + 1 = 3   transformation from that point on reads

$$f - 2 + 1 = 3$$

|
three
re
t ree
t ree
t re at
thre at

(a − 2
e − 5 + 2 = 7
h − 2   7e + 6t = 13et
r − 5
t − 4 + 2 = 6

thirteenet
+   te n
+ th r ee
+ thirt   y
56yet
5 + 6 = 11
&1 + 1 = 2
= resolved yet

The Room:

arrow

      a row of r's

sparrow or song
           bird

•

sunlight
      s's unlight
darkness
        where the walls hide
inside the d
        its belly
the sun is born in
its ark
ness

•

leafy leaving
the room leavened
air rises
        la salle
l'air

when s is all e
we see or scream
the hiss moving into terror

green
     the colour of
le
  (the)
a
  (un)
f

f's ear

•

a distaste with r
ug
     it is blue & yellow

it is green

       r's a is
the sun
       (un s but very r)

its age is anger
it is not itself when it runs

this has been a description of one r
ug
     in the middle of my floor

•

ellie l e
particular lady la d

tender belly

a w o man
is where the woman am

lovely

•

'b.o. is ok'

book

'what about bad breath?'

'it's cold eating h's'

if p is s
piss on it

'shh'

•

suppose L am P
is light possible

is s a witch
when science is the itch scratches it

a ch in the air
next to where it stands

i scratch my chin

science?
            or just my hand?

march 8/73

a little song

for george bowering

a
blake
lake

keats
eats

shelley
hell
he

et
rossetti

love song 1

as many times as i have thot to love you
acknowledging the permission your actions grant
to enter the imagined landscape of your body
taut breasts & bellied pubic hair
i have done nothing but think of you
naked as you bathe
followed your movements across the floor
behind the door i have feared to open
you have left unlocked for me
who would have & would not have possession of the key
not knowing what value you place upon it
not knowing the secret places where you dwell
darker worlds your eyes warn of
where the bed changes unpredictable as the sea
tossing you up into the arms of lovers
with what fears of drowning you have never mentioned
tho i see them there
wanting you as it seems i always do
trembling each time i've held you
                                   & never spoken

probable systems 4

this one's for james joyce in his worst bummer

faith
= 6 + 1 + 9 + 20 + 8
= 44
= 8 + 15 + 16 + 5
= hope

probable systems 5

dante's formula

$$HOl\mathcal{E} + 298 = H\mathcal{E}ll$$
$$H\mathcal{E}ll \times lO = H\mathcal{E}llO$$
$$H\mathcal{E}llO - \mathcal{E}llO = HOOOO$$

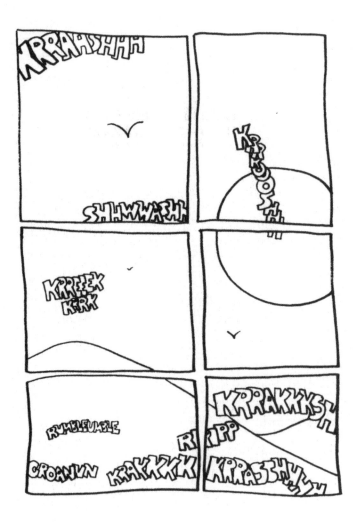

Crossing

semen of seamen's sons in this sea son

steve sits down

saint eve /
        / ning
bridge bell rings
changing the seasons

in the wake the waves break over the wood
going down in the tide's rising

ground swell

•

a boat

a bot thing

a singing
like a whale

a wind &
a windlass
winding

•

the cut off the stern
the slash

lashed by the s
break & curve

swerving

as the waves were

•

nova to new

the translation

'carried into heaven without death'

trans-atlantic trance state

e/lation

•

sun's moon
earth's son

eclipse

'i am in my grandmother's shadow'

if the E clips the E
it is F or H

turning round

o

•

p or t

q r s

wave q are
            (blessed)

crossing ended
N dead

my last name

no family ties to cling to

only these roads across such bodies as exist

wakes left

       write

ing

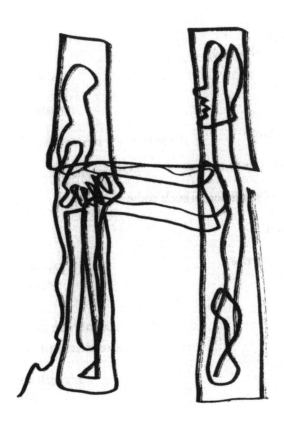

Blizzard

head cold

an old c vitamin
gone astray

a stray A
rays from a saint's head
RA's 'why'

HE (a.d. 1973) admonishes me
for my ignorance

march 17 1973

triangulation

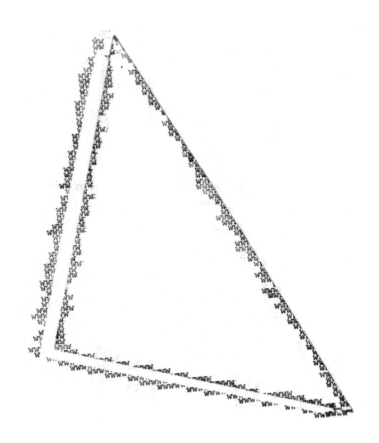

march 23/72

A Study of Context: H

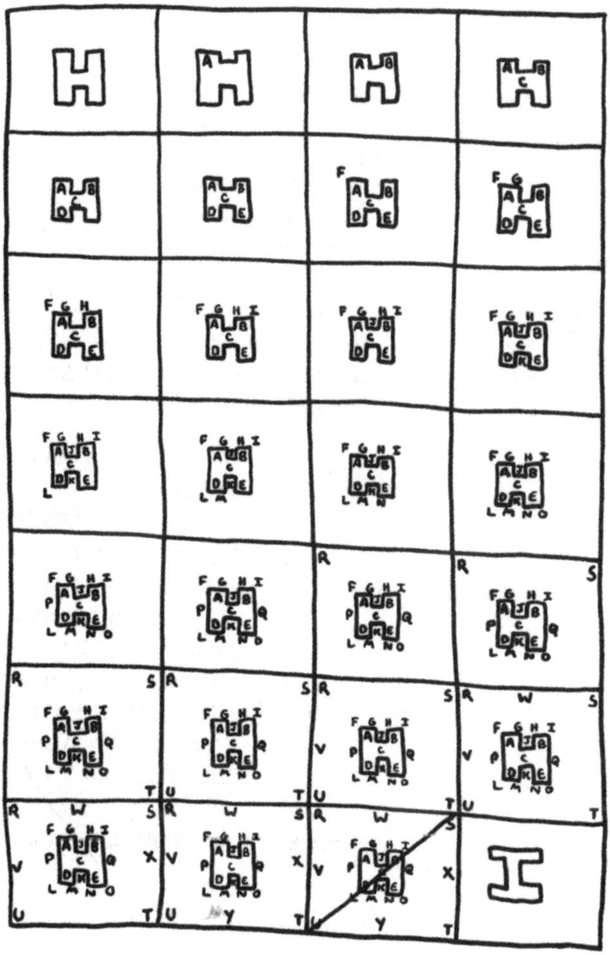

december 72

the riddle

sunny days
s is un n

why

      an s day
is not like any other day

a day is
a d & a y
& i am s

sunny days
i am un n

why

                                        april 24/73

for steve

an and and an an   a this and that   his this is that hat or her error
   now it is winter & spring comes   that day   i walked towards
the the from the a   the other way
   woods &

              to encompass the world
              to take it in
              inside that outside
              outside that in
              to be real
              one thing beside the other

later there is are   that was to be   a sense in which a saint is was &
will be   so the issue's this   this as is his claim on the present
tension past & future always the question of what to do each step
altering your choices

voice as song
              speech is
to belong to
form as an expression of dilemma
conceptualization placing you on the brink of dissolution
you make a choice
narrow the distance between
the tree as it is & the word 'tree'
between the object & the object
as the you can be the me
we are (as pronouns) each other
nouns divide
hide behind that name we are given

late night outside the room
book beside the window
words inside
                written

as they are
objects in the world we live in
carry us far
            ther a
way
      from
            each
                  other
                        than
                              they
                                    should

probable systems 6

rainy afternoon

*Z – A = Y

Y + E = ?
Z – (A + T) = E
E + (Z – A) = ?   Y ? E ? Y ? ?
T + E = Y
E + (E + T) = ?
2E + T = ?   QUESTION MARKS **

remove Y & E

???? – E = QUSTION MARKS
(???? – E) – Y = (QUS(CHYON) MARKS) – Y = QUSCHON MARKS

Addenda:

Y + E = DO = 2o = 6E
E + (Z – A) = E + Y = (see above)
E + (E + T) = E + Y = (see below)
2E + T = J + T = DO = 2o = 6E

---

* initial combinations thru random samplings of memory traces
** at this point letters could be systematically deleted by whatever means necessary   choose letters at random & see what they yield

from CATULLUS poem XXVIII

Piss on his committees, cohorts in inanities
apt as sarcasm & as expeditious,
Verani was too optimistic my Fabulle,
who put the geritol in his rum? satisfied? me?! with such
vapid frigid rascals and too listless women?
Damn him as well in tableaus patterned at Lucelli's
expense, dumb monkey, who sucks the mothers'
pretties for refreshment and yells 'Oh –
oh mommy, give me that godly supper –
to taste the trickle in my lips makes you my master'
(said with big eyes, parents being first
cause (such minor nihilistic truths
are farts)). the prick's a noble friend!
the voices of men milking gods with
their teeth are as appropriate as Romulus's remarks.

love song 2

just once to say 'i love you' all the feeling felt
to dwell inside the words as they are spoken
(not broken on the tongue by my intent
conscious or otherwise
to hold back in speech each feeling
behind the syntax of my own attention
naming song what never sings
but is a circling in my tension round you)
that desire to 'say' totally
in gesture as in word
all that i do feel for you
locked up in hesitations i give you as poems

I.T.A.N.U.T.S. 3

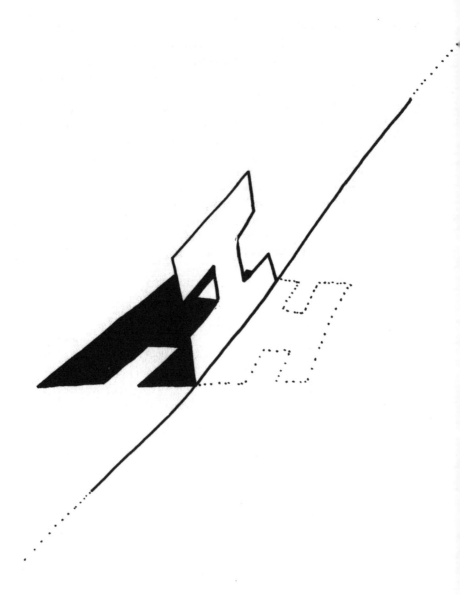

december 72

probable systems 7

base issue for the late Marilyn Monroe

A + B + C + D + E + F + G + H + I + J + K + L + M + N + O + P +

Q + R + S + T + U + V + W + X + Y + Z = MM

trio

given

prose

~~poetry~~ :× 3 = H
~~ror~~

&

poetry

~~prose~~ ÷ 3 = I
~~try~~

then

prose = ⅓ H & poetry = 31

since H = 8 & I = 9
then
prose = 2⅔ & poetry = 27

BUT

since poetry − (oetry) + (rose) = prose
& since o = 15 e = 5 t = 20 r = 18 y = 25 & s = 19
then 27 − 83 + 57 = 2⅔
& 1 = 2⅔

similarly: prose − rose + oetry = 27
yielding 2⅔ − 57 + 83 = 27
or 28⅔ = 27

subtracting the smaller # from the larger # in both of the above cases
we arrive at a value of 1⅔ the measured difference between prose &
poetry

commentary:

another way of figuring arrives at a different answer
since poetry = 99 & prose = 73 then the difference between them
is 26 or the number of letters in the alphabet   since this method
appears more precise what is the value of the first answer arrived

at   starting from the basic premise that H & I follow one another in the alphabet having a difference in value of 1 (poetry & prose placed in the same base have a difference of 10)   the relationship between them is perfect   by turning I one counter clock-wise position it becomes H   by turning H one counter clock-wise position it becomes I   (C&U M&W N&Z are the only other letters whose relationships to one another are at all similar   however none of these are as perfect in relation to one another as H&I)   in the premise the fractioning or multiplying of poetry & prose by 3 (the number of the mother continent MU (MUse?)) is an expression in mathematical terms of the effect of cosmic forces on the writing   (the initial relationship is demonstrated by the transforming of poetry into prose using the alphabetic replacement system prior to multiplying & then the reverse prior to dividing   prose is multiplied by 3 because the cosmic forces are less present in prose since the consciousness of the writer tends to intrude to a much greater degree   thus to equalize the equalizable factors as much as possible poetry is subsequently divided by 3)   since the relationship between H&I is the closest approximation in pure language terms of the relationship between poetry & prose by using them as equivalents we arrive at a purer mathematical description   both answers are right   26 comes closest to the traditional english grammar ideal   1⅔ is purer because it brings into play the flux in the world of the writer & its relationship to writing   it is interesting to note that the value of I is a multiple of 3 thus arriving at 27 as the value of poetry as opposed to ⅜ as the value of prose   note the simplicity & directness of the relationship between poetry & the cosmic forces   further to this in the final transformation in both cases 1⅔ is actually an expression of the margin of difference in transformational writing i.e. when one is moving from poetry into prose or vice versa   this is to say that 1⅔ is a measure of their difference in terms of borderblur writing as opposed to (as is the case with 26) an expression of their gross difference if you do not try bringing the two things together   1⅔ is an expression of the degree of flux in actual transformational writing

I.T.A.N.U.T.S. 6

H as future Alpha as unknown factor

love song

for margaret avison

the le the the an a année annie saint ani slaus   that that or this
this   what what asked   the's in confusion   some a's   a train
passes thru   or an or   an an   standing   & after sitting standing
    (yesterday this would've been different   tomorrow it will not be
the same)   & after standing sitting   after sitting sitting   not
sitting   & then you came

from CATULLUS poem LXI

Colic Heliconian
culture, genius Uranus,
who rapes sheep & drinks
virgin piss, o hymen of Hymen,
    o Hymen's hymen;

such tempers flare
love relents,
let us cap it flamboyantly, mile
high towers, new gestures
    under Socrates' moon;

exquisite hilarity of death,
coincidental opening of
the wedded vulva,
smell of human penises, shit
    on sheep's feet.

name me a man whose colon dilates,
as Venus's did
at the sight of Phrygius
crying, how good to feel
    you come inside me,

flushed with the smell of
myrtle trees on Asia's rim
where Hadrian could've died
ludicrous as it seems
    for lack of love.

what age, however fierce,
purged of Thespia's colloquialisms
now that he lies ruptured in the Aonian caves,
could tolerate the nymphomaniacs
    frigged Aganippe to death.

how dominated by dullness we are.
knowing nothing of love,
renouncing what meaning remains,
we lose our heads amid the implications
    of errors stacking up like logs.

there is no single item, no intact
virgin, that on discovery
doesn't die. agitation is the modern
deceit, o hymen of Hymen,
    o Hymen's hymen.

december 72

from CATULLUS poem IIa

Damn grateful I am when ferreting bellies
pernicky as the golden hole fussing my lips,
when this zone dissolves around my prick.

the game

ten N is
B's all

court

short day or
stroke

        saint roke
fort
    undressing
sings
     under the s   a
no t
    her language

c our t's retort

Pastoral

for Mike Ondaatje

talking about strawberries all of the time

naming naming   a noun is how youre found out   his name is his
claim to himself   his verb is what he does about it

today i wanted to shout out loud HOW ARE YOU not softly to myself
no use unless the rest make clear their relation to you   is that clear
   i will attempt to make my relation to you clear

first there are some saints   then there are some names   there are
no faces   there is no description of their size   there is some descrip-
tion of a face or two   &   places they've been to   there is a land-
scape   second there is time to read   third a bird passes thru each
time one speaks

       voice: i want to set a scene with no explanation of my name
                 there is a plain thru which a river flows   it is very old &
                 folds & folds & folds   now there is a cloud hiding
                 the sun   this could be a description of anyone at anytime
                 the difference is that this description rymes
2nd voice: i want to talk about strawberries all of the time   is it
                 very boring   there is a pouring of milk folding over red
                 berries in a bowl & a face that smiles because it is so
                 later there will be no description of any noun   later
                 there will be less signs of frowning & more happiness
                 lately everything glows
   1st voice: there has been too much statement   where there is
                 statement there is no discovery   there must be some
                 statements   some things have been discovered
2nd voice: that's enough uncovered   later there will be much
                 more   that is not a promise   do not promise more
                 than you can deliver

1st voice:

> & the clouds flow the cloud flows
> like like like like like
> unlikely tho   over everything
> one sings
> liking strawberries very much
> fresh from the garden
> when the sky is blue &
> your lady is your lover is beside you
> just so

•

madness is language is how you use it   if you are not mad you use it
one way   if you are mad you use it another way   these are not
categories   there are many ways of both ways

   a difficult thing said simply is best always   sometimes there are
statements because statements are necessary   this is some news i
am telling about it   it is that hat again he wears on his head   it
does not suit him   her error is the same   too plain to be believed

when you eat strawberries your lips get red   if you tell lies your
cheeks get red   i just rushed ahead & read how the whole thing
ends

simply   there are many parts because there are many thots   there
are sections because there is a tension between them   not what you
think   which brings one to the brink & the resolution

•

strawberries julia are best fresh better than frozen   straw barries &
tin men & cowardly lions & let us continue the book of oz again

resemblances

tenses
          & past
participles

nipples are red as strawberries

a list is just sense

i rushed ahead to here
& the whole thing ended
as intended

is that clear

   •

now
let me say this

he said it

good then it's over

let us sleep   let us be   i was so happy just eating my strawberries

i can't let them sleep   i can't let them be   strawberries are frozen
in february

   •

now let me say this again

he said it again

is it over

no

it occurs to me

it just occurred

it is my sense of self your selves deferred to a better judgement

it is sound & a startled sense of what is

tis

•

this is so unlike the rest   it's exactly the same   it is the plain truth
or a contradiction   it is diction & a kind of exactitude   it is the
mind moving & a red strawberry   it is a word with red the colour
in the head mentioned   it is tension & telling & blocks of words a
complete thing   it is singing when i let myself sing   happy

•

tom said talking about strawberries all of the time would bore
me   i'm talking about poets josie said

•

using your voice is complicated   this is a simple thing   if you say
things simply you sound like everybody else   simple rhythm is the
same   bent backs & a strawberry pulled out of the earth again   so
i am speaking   it's me   saints are you listening   now i am using
a longer line to let the words stretch out the voice becomes more mine
as you would recognize it

> & the vision between
> the eyes & the world
> focussed on its skin
> you can't see

except to say it is this combination of words is me   these signs   as
long as this book exists   longer than the red strawberry

problem: find $\sqrt{\text{logic}}$ to nearest whole letter
since logic = AU & AU = DG (base j)
then $\sqrt{\text{logic}}$ = DG (base j)

performing all necessary operations in base j then

```
              F. F C
       F√DG.oooo
              CI
   ABF    H oo
           G EF
   ACBC    DDoo
            C I F I
            DCA
```

rounding off to the nearest whole letter we have a given value for the $\sqrt{\text{logic}}$ as G in both base j & base alphabet

---

COMMENTARY:
            what troubled me with this system was the abrupt
initial statement since base alphabet is not necessarily a readily acces-
sible concept   further the whole process of trying to pin something
down exactly only serves to reconfirm Heisenberg's PRINCIPLE OF
UNCERTAINTY i.e. that the more exact you try to be in your description
of something the farther you move away from the reality of its existence
& thus the rounding off to the nearest whole letter   the concept of
whole letter is itself an interesting one which will be gone into in
greater detail in a future system since if you have H & if you have I
what are the fractional letters in between them & what do they
express

probable systems 10

a time machine

time is all & everything   everything is part of time & time is part
of everything   we think of time as a linear event moving thus:

————————————A——————————B——————————C—————————

                                              if our life span is A
to C then there are those whose life spans are A to B or A to Z as well
as those for whom it is simply A or simply Z   if our A is another man
woman or things A to Z & another's A to C then we are another man
woman or thing's A   thus we could conceive of a series of parallel
linear events

                    ——————————————

                         ——————————————

        ——————————

    ——————————————————

      ——————————

                                ——————

                              each representing a different
life a different sense or passage of time   but time doesn't travel in
parallel lines   time is part of everything & thus its motion is in all
directions simultaneously

given: three time spans beginning at the same point in time (say
january 1, 1967)

problem: set up three points of intersection
solution:

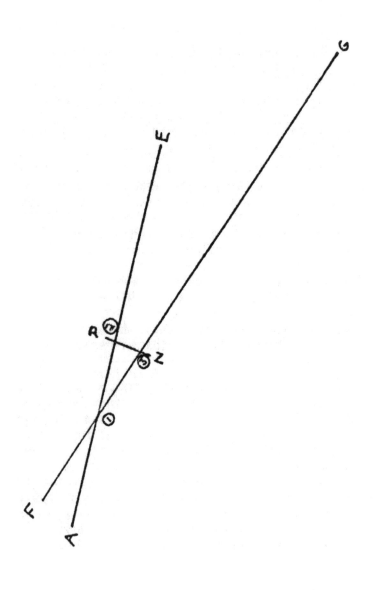

problem: given that E is the year 1975 what are the dates of
             intersection in the solution to the previous problem

if E = 1975 then 1 year = ½ inch since A to E is 4 inches long therefore
since both F & R also begin at 1967 by measuring the length of F–G
& R–Z we discover the value of G to be the year 1978 & Z to be the
year 1968

therefore by measuring the point at which on each line the intersections
occur we can arrive at the dates of intersection

intersection point 1:   january 1969 on line F–G
                          on line A–E may 15 1969

intersection point 2:   november 15 1970 on line A–E
                          april 1 1967 on line R–Z

intersection point 3:   august 15 1970 on line F–G
                          october 1 1967 on line R–Z

thus on october 1 1967 R–Z actually travelled forward to august 15
1970 intersecting with F–G   at the same time F–G of course travelled
into the past to october 1967   similarly on april 1 1967 R–Z travelled
forward to november 15 1970 at the same time that A–E travelled
back to april 1 1967 & so on   thus we can see that time travel is
already taking place all the time all around us & that since the number
of linear events & hence the number of intersections is infinite all of
us are always travelling back & forth in time   the self that occupies
occupied will occupy each particle of your life line is travelling in time
simultaneously   this has the effect of cancelling out awareness of
time travel   the real problem here then in the creation of a time
machine is of making oneself aware that one is already travelling in
time   it is a problem with the preceptual* system   the question
becomes if we are travelling in time why aren't we aware of it   it is
perhaps over obvious to state that a sense of *self* is equated with a
sense of oneness & that to be aware at any given moment of one's
self travelling in time is to be aware of all one's *selves* travelling in
time & thus one's sense of oneness is threatened by the perception of
a multiplicity of selves all at different ages etc. travelling simultane-
ously in time   since that sense of oneness is therefore threatened

---

* i.e. the precepts that inform the perceptual system and the pre-awarenesses
whose sum equals perception

with annhilation with complete disintegration upon the acknowledgement of this perception this perception is not acknowledged   since it is also true that if the number of points of intersection is infinite then on one of the jumps forwards or backwards one will visit a time before or after one lived then to acknowledge the perception of time travelling would mean to be aware of selves gradually disintegrating in the absence of a state of being   needless to say such a perception would be too traumatic for one's sense of oneness   these then are the factors that stand in the way of our conscious acknowledged use of the already existing time machine (consciousness would mean the chance to choose which point you intersected with & for how long) & explain why it hasn't been discovered earlier   it now remains for someone to find the key which will unlock it

october 1971

A Study of Context 2: S into H

from CATULLUS poem LXXXVIII

Whose face is this, Gelli, comes unmarked by sores
    pure & objecting to lifting her tunic?
whose face is this, father, no sin has marred?
    how much would she fetch from susceptible sellers?
how much more susceptible, o Gelli, to this Tethys
    this nymph of the Ocean?
nothing's worse than quick quim sellers, packagers of beauty,
    nothing's so deadly so upsets the heart.

I.T.A.N.U.T.S. 9

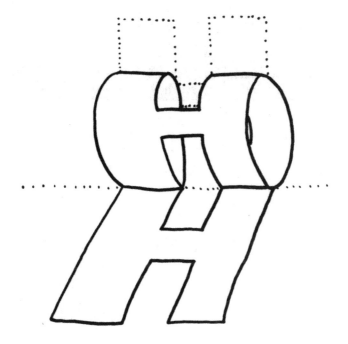

december 72

L.T. 5

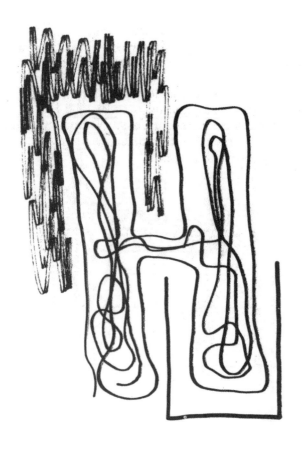

from CATULLUS poem XXXII

My beautiful my sweet Ipsitilla,
my delicious leopard,
nubile & wet as the mediterranean.
and so sensuous, so lewd in her adieus,
never limited to table-top observances,
she bares her tits for our libations,
sad such noblemen as us must leave,
hoping her future can include us.
but if age should wear her beauty, even as statues are worn,
no prince or wolf or satyr will come home
to pierce her tunic with his prick.

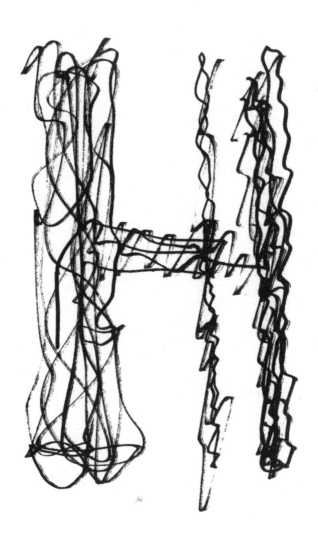

probable systems 11:

hierarchy of alphabetic naming

1) pure vowels

   a
   e
   i
   o
   u

2) consonant/vowel

   b
   c
   d
   g
   j
   k
   p
   q
   t
   v
   y

3) vowel/consonant

   f
   l
   m
   n
   r
   s
   x

4) consonant/vowel/consonant (Canadian pronunciation)

   z

5) pure consonants

   h
   w

probable systems 12

alphabetical bases: a t

	B	C	D	E	F	G	H	I	J	K	L	M	N	O	P
A	A	A	A	A	A	A	A	A	A	A	A	A	A	A	A
B	A□	B	B	B	B	B	B	B	B	B	B	B	B	B	B
C	AA	A□	C	C	C	C	C	C	C	C	C	C	C	C	C
D	A□□	AA	A□	D	D	D	D	D	D	D	D	D	D	D	D
E	A□A	AB	AA	A□	E	E	E	E	E	E	E	E	E	E	E
F	AA□	B□	AB	AA	A□	F	F	F	F	F	F	F	F	F	F
G	AAA	BA	AC	AB	AA	A□	G	G	G	G	G	G	G	G	G
H	A□□□	BB	B□	AC	AB	AA	A□	H	H	H	H	H	H	H	H
I	A□□A	A□□	BA	AD	AC	AB	AA	A□	I	I	I	I	I	I	I
J	A□A□	A□A	BB	B□	AD	AC	AB	AA	A□	J	J	J	J	J	J
K	A□AA	A□B	BC	BA	AE	AD	AC	AB	AA	A□	K	K	K	K	K
L	AA□□	AA□	C□	BB	B□	AE	AD	AC	AB	AA	A□	L	L	L	L
M	AA□A	AAA	CA	BC	BA	AF	AE	AD	AC	AB	AA	A□	M	M	M
N	AAA□	AAB	CB	BD	BB	B□	AF	AE	AD	AC	AB	AA	A□	N	N
O	AAAA	AB□	CC	C□	BC	BA	AG	AF	AE	AD	AC	AB	AA	A□	O
P	A□□□□	ABA	A□□	CA	BD	BB	B□	AG	AF	AE	AD	AC	AB	AA	A□
Q	A□□□A	ABB	A□A	CB	BE	BC	BA	AH	AG	AF	AE	AD	AC	AB	AA
R	A□□A□	B□□	A□B	CC	C□	BD	BB	B□	AH	AG	AF	AE	AD	AC	AB
S	A□□AA	B□A	A□C	CD	CA	BE	BC	BA	AI	AH	AG	AF	AE	AD	AC
T	A□A□□	B□B	AA□	D□	CB	BF	BD	BB	B□	AI	AH	AG	AF	AE	AD
U	A□A□A	BA□	AAA	DA	CC	C□	BE	BC	BA	AJ	AI	AH	AG	AF	AE
V	A□AA□	BAA	AAB	DB	CD	CA	BF	BD	BB	B□	AJ	AI	AH	AG	AF
W	A□AAA	BAB	AAC	DC	CE	CB	BG	BE	BC	BA	AK	AJ	AI	AH	AG
X	AA□□□	BB□	AB□	DD	D□	CC	C□	BF	BD	BB	B□	AK	AJ	AI	AH
Y	AA□□A	BBA	ABA	A□□	DA	CD	CA	BG	BE	BC	BA	AL	AK	AJ	AI
Z	AA□A□	BBB	ABB	A□A	DB	CE	CB	BH	BF	BD	BB	B□	AL	AK	AJ

* in this table □ denotes an empty place

Q	R	S	T	U	V	W	X	Y	Z
A	A	A	A	A	A	A	A	A	A
B	B	B	B	B	B	B	B	B	B
C	C	C	C	C	C	C	C	C	C
D	D	D	D	D	D	D	D	D	D
E	E	E	E	E	E	E	E	E	E
F	F	F	F	F	F	F	F	F	F
G	G	G	G	G	G	G	G	G	G
H	H	H	H	H	H	H	H	H	H
I	I	I	I	I	I	I	I	I	I
J	J	J	J	J	J	J	J	J	J
K	K	K	K	K	K	K	K	K	K
L	L	L	L	L	L	L	L	L	L
M	M	M	M	M	M	M	M	M	M
N	N	N	N	N	N	N	N	N	N
O	O	O	O	O	O	O	O	O	O
P	P	P	P	P	P	P	P	P	P
A□	Q	Q	Q	Q	Q	Q	Q	Q	Q
AA	A□	R	R	R	R	R	R	R	R
AB	AA	A□	S	S	S	S	S	S	S
AC	AB	AA	A□	T	T	T	T	T	T
AD	AC	AB	AA	A□	U	U	U	U	U
AE	AD	AC	AB	AA	A□	V	V	V	V
AF	AE	AD	AC	AB	AA	A□	W	W	W
AG	AF	AE	AD	AC	AB	AA	A□	X	X
AH	AG	AF	AE	AD	AC	AB	AA	A□	Y
AI	AH	AG	AF	AE	AD	AC	AB	AA	A□

I.T.A.N.U.T.S.12

december 72

love song 3

when there are no roles left
when he has finally come
back to the fearful point he had fled from
where all pain & futility he has felt dwells
knowing the hell she knelt in
& yet gave birth
                         he is torn between praise & scorn
the wanting that has screamed inside him
afraid to face again
the emptiness he felt calling her name
in a darkened room the mind inhabits as its own
knowing the love he felt for her she could never return
burned up by the passion of her own dead desires
no life for the living form crawled out of her
who still, today, moves under the sway of that hunger
will not be consoled
no matter what arms he finds to hold him
what nipples his mouth closes round
because he is older & the wanting will not make it so

probable systems 13:

text & deduction

song

s on g
or simply on
as s can be

ass scan
(looking both ways)
s in e
        wave goodbye
a w
    a y
an s or
rowing faster
f as t
s as k at o on the map face
tracing the line all the way thru
these lines are so long
the s e (l in e) s are (is) so l on g

---

if l is on g
& l is in e
& since s is in e (as we have already seen)
& s is on g
then s & l ∈ e & e is on g

now since e is on g & f lies between e & g
then the meaning of the alphabetic sequence 'e f g' becomes clear

april 1973

Moonth

nomoonday
marsday
mercuryday
jupiterday
venusday
saturnday
sunday
halfmoonday
marsday
mercuryday
jupiterday
venusday
saturnday
sunday
moonday
marsday
mercuryday
jupiterday
venusday
saturnday
sunday
halfmoonday
marsday
mercuryday
jupiterday
venusday
saturnday
sunday
nomoonday

from CATULLUS poem XLIX

<u>Dissertation on Romulus's nepotism:</u>
'What cunts quote that fart' Marcus Tulli
(note the postulate is no grunting anus)

december 72

Toth 4

Angel of Mercy

summer 73

lament

cruelty   the land was
harsh   as is told you
a barren island marguerite de roberval was marooned on
in the mouth of the saint lawrence river
by her uncle
viceroy of canada
for having fallen in love with
a poor man
              he escaped the ship &
swam to join her

this is the first european family we know of
one child is born to them
there on the isle of demons
so called because the wind howled over the rocks
drowned in sound the three of them

later she is rescued
returned to france
her husband & her child dead of famine
rode out the storm her mind broken
by such cruelty as should never come again
out of this land to haunt us

  •

innocence
         in a sense
begins on   the outcrop

that we had it & lost it (maybe)
that we never had it (closer to the truth)

that we could all be to this day
marguerite de roberval's fantasy of company
alone on the isle of demons
dreaming of a country full of people
a land you could grow food in
starving to death
human howling in the elemental grief

landscape: 1

for thomas a. clark

alongthehorizongrewanunbrokenlineoftrees

probable systems 15

division of the signified

Toth 5

The Wedding

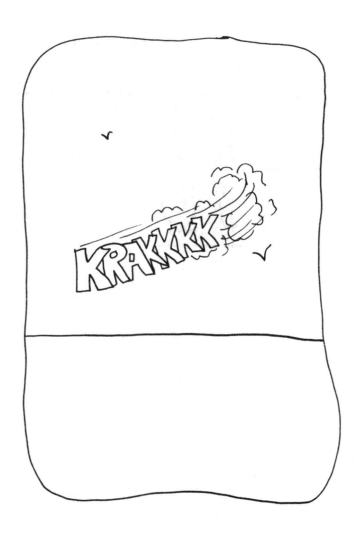

I.T.A.N.U.T.S. 14

december 72

from CATULLUS poem LI

Ill am I, paralyzed, whom God did hurt.
ill, suffering, a rare meal for gods
who sit, idle & adverse,
    watching & listening.

sweet ridicule, misery that ominous
spirits sense as meat, now, too simply,
Lesbia, that pixie, eats me for supper
    with her golden voice.

language speaks its torture, tenuous sub-articulations
inflame my madness, sonnets of supplicants
tinkle in the air, gem-like talking to
    light my darkness.

Opium – Catullus: to be is to be molested
open & exultant in my numb genesis:
opium & rage pry & beat at
    my fading sight.

south

a bus's stop

a b
us s's top

it is covered over

a wagon or
a bat

his hand
on top of that
one i call mine

m in e
it is not me
as i just said

days the hand seems
so far from
the head

the HE AND the HA

No Date

getting impatient
because the bus is late

Travelling

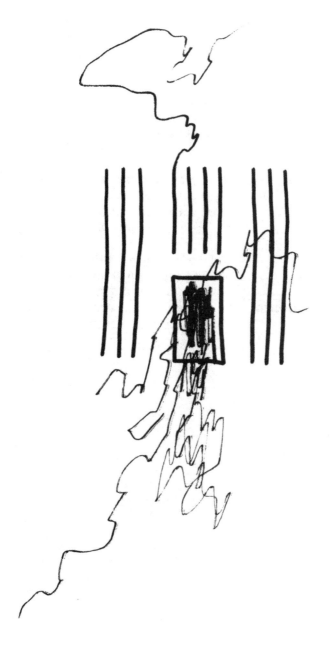

Probable systems 16:

device for measuring the signified

Howdy Dewdney: a broadway poem

for Chris Dewdney & Bob Fones

lead around the room by my head

nothing is 'like' something else
it likes it
assimilation
assumption of   qualities the
character-
          istics

(we make it home thru the streets at 2 a.m.
drunk
          streetlight don't like the moon
their chorus
                    music against the sphere
the windshield being glass
glasses could be part of the image
what we look thru
                    from
my 'point-of-view' is an illusion)

absolutes

absolutions

abstract solutions to abstract problems making for an abstract
                                                            day

or night

                    'just an abstract guy
                    under abstract skies
                    singing abstract songs about you'

                    october 20/2:20 a.m.

december 72

‖ **Zygon** (zəi·gɒn). Pl. **zyga** (zəi·gă). [mod.L., ad. Gr. ζυγόν yoke.]

1. *Anat.* The bar or stem connecting the two branches of an H-shaped fissure (*zygal fissure*) of the brain.

Zygal (zəi·găl), *a. Anat.* [f. ZYGON + -AL.] Pertaining to or having a zygon.

1886 B. G. WILDER in *Jrnl. Nerv. & Mental Dis.* June 304 The complete or typical condition of a zygal fissure is like two y's joined by their stems, .. or, viewed from the side, like an expanded H.

HALF OF THE
H's DESTROYED
EVERY YEAR ARE
DESTROYED THRU
DROPPAGE!!

art facts
a book of contexts

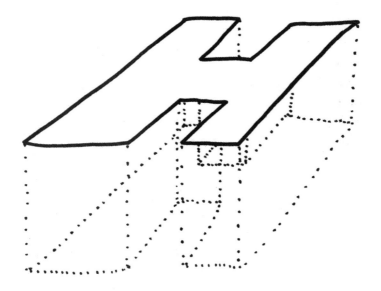

طلب ما يفوت لا يترك ما يدركه بعضه

Arabic saying: 'If the "whole" cannot be obtained,
let not the greater part of it be left unmentioned.'

for Victor

'Time is our error.'

bird and
          breaking the clear calm
beaver's head
               over the water
i'm glad to see you
                  walking this
held out his hand
              green & foreign land to be
living in troubled times my mind fills quickly
too much to say
            your brown skin & dark eyes
too many friends being hounded to death by
this sickness
            thot we'd raise jerusalem here
ripple this surface with the wind

dreamed anthology 1

a poem by George Bowering
(dreamt circa 1964/65)

islands in the mist

in the grey fog

out from the coastline

– fragment only
possible title: 'Coast Poems'

Ocean Song

EBBtide.

tidetide

E B B

E B B

tidetide

2nd Movement

tide   tide
ebb   ebb   ebb
ebb   ebb   ebb
tide   tide
tideebbbbbbbbbb

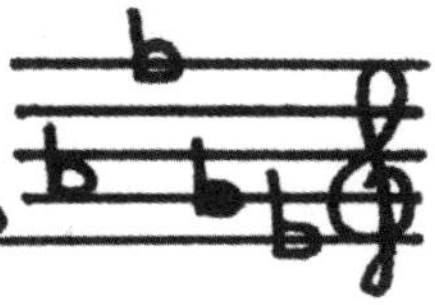

3rd Movement

tide
tied

ebb

4th Movement

tideebbtideebbebbtideebbebbebbtide

tie   ding   hy

ebb

              ebb

6th Movement

probable systems 17

the circumference of the spoken word

any word is made up of a sequence of lip movements during which the word is sounded.

EXAMPLE:

W   O R   D

thus (if we are to take the title of this particular system literally) the circumference of 'word' as it is spoken would be the total of the circumference of each lip opening during its speaking.

the circumference of 'w' + the circumference of 'or'
+ the circumference of 'd' = the circumference of
'word'

we can propose then a formula which would give us the circumference of any spoken word.

$$W = C_1 + C_2 + C_3 \text{ etc}$$

where W is the circumference of any word, C the circumference of the mouth opening at the apex of its particular phonemic movement & where 1,2,3 etc indicates the particular phoneme in terms of its place in the relevant speech sequence.

COMMENTARY:

immediately upon completing the first draft of this system, which i had tentatively titled THE CIRCUMFERENCE OF THE WORD, i realized the necessity for the more accurate titling which now accompanies it because of two elements: 1) ventriloquism & 2) printed language. these two elements gave rise to two subsequent systems: PROBABLE SYSTEMS 21, the weight of speech (for Rube Goldberg) & PROBABLE SYSTEMS 24, physical contexts of human speech. it is worth pointing out tho that this system is hopelessly inadequate because of the variables present in any group of human speakers. the best one could hope for is a broad enough sampling to enable us to arrive at a statistical approximation of what the circumference of a particular word would be.

attempted diagnoses

s s c k
i i c k
s i c c
s i k k
i i k k
s s k k
s s c c
i i c c
i i i c
s i i i
s s s i
s s s c
s s s k
k k k s
s c c c
c c c s
c s c c
c c s c
k c s c
k k s c
k k s k
k s k k
i s k k
i s i k
i s i i
i i s i
s i s i
s i s s
s s i s
s s c s
s k s s
s s k s
s k c s
k s s c
k i i c
i k c i
i c k i
i s k i
i k s i

isci
icsi
kick
kcik
kisk
ksik
ksck
kcsk
ckic
cikc
cskc
cksc
cisc

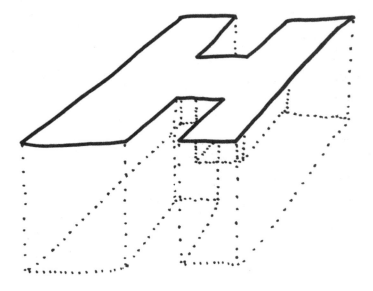

December 1972

probable systems 18

dream & commentaries as a probable source
(with additional research including Probable Systems 30*)*

Friday August 17th, 1973

    dreamt i'd returned to wildwood park in winnipeg. they'd torn down all the houses and trees in the centre of the u-shaped section we used to live in, including our old house, and covered the whole thing with gravel. at the bottom of the u an apartment building was going up. i started crying & screaming because they were going to destroy the trees and the parkland between the u-sections.

COMMENTARY 1: POEM (AUGUST 17TH, 1973)

drove east thru the kawarthas toward verona
burleigh falls behind us
where i thot i saw the drowned child
feet & arms wedged beneath the rocks

awaking that morning
dreams of the red river flood
where we'd lived   H-section   wildwood park
lifetime pursuits explained
                        mysterious other train of thot
drawing me east out of the dreamed landscape
'was' is all i 'saw'

H circa 1950
i can never go back again
before H
        A to G
winnipeg manitoba
w in m
        i in H
its section?

'look for the big H'   Harvey comics
didackdick tracing   passages of a thot
the facts stack backwards
                the connections

origins of a quest
was that how it was when they wandered east
shields emblazoned with the family crest
under the grail's holy influence?
the children who had gone before them
                                    to be sold into slavery or
dead beside the highway
where the next crusade would find them

child of H
children of Holy Matrimony
M into 3
Holy Trinity of suffering
host out of Ghost
fed nothing for their vision but lies
God's host betrayed
it was lost love they thot to find

despair thru the laurentians
north towards noranda
the chaos is man's
the perfect plan is not planned
that space that line run parallel yet meet

H
    crude symbol of the bridging
a re-perception of what was once unitas
I
    H
      S

COMMENTARY 2: AUTOBIOGRAPHICAL NOTE

in 1950 i was living with my mother, father, sister and two brothers
in H-section, one of a number of u-shaped sections in an area of
Winnipeg called Wildwood Park. in the spring of that year, the Red
River flooded its banks, creating in the process a major disaster, and
we, and thousands of others like us, were forced to move out until the
disaster had passed and the clean-up that followed was finished. i
have a vague memory of my Mom, my sister and me being carried
away in a boat across areas i was used to walking over. we went to live
with relatives, first in Saskatoon and then in Calgary.

H-section was where i first learned my ABC's, and one of the things i learned at the same time was how to find my way home. if i was walking from one direction i knew that right after G-section was H-section and H was where home was. if i was walking from another direction i knew that I came just after H so that H-section had to be the next one i'd come to. and of course i could always cut thru the middle of the Park and jump from one letter to another in all kinds of patterns, just as a way of getting home.

i hated the period when we were up-rooted, sleeping in borrowed beds under cramped conditions. it was, as they say, traumatic. and i was over-joyed when we finally moved back, six months later. we got our dad to show us how high the flood water had risen (to just below the window of my sister's and mine's second floor bedroom) and then had him nail a little wooden donkey to the spot to mark what had happened. sometimes my sister and i would try to imagine the house under all that water, as tho we had lived there, in it (under it), thru the whole flood.

but something happened to me after that flood. when the water receded i had changed. i had become H obsessed. i collected the Hardy Boys and Harvey Comics (whose slogan was 'look for the Big H!' & who published, among other titles, *Dick Tracy Comics*). i loved Baby Huey and the comic my brother drew 'SUPERHOG' (which circulated widely for a number of years in its single hand-drawn version and then disappeared). H. i couldn't get enough of it. and of course it was still H-section and, for a time, Home. all of which i forgot or, at least, never connected with my adult interest, until August 17th, 1973, when i had the above dream, me with my (part) German roots, discovering the origin in my Hunconscious of one of the I's obsessions.

COMMENTARY 3: "PATAPHYSICAL IMPLICATIONS OF DEEPER SOURCES (RETURN TO WINNIPEG, FEBRUARY 7TH, 1978.*)

INTRO: the accompanying map, 'found' during a trip to Winnipeg, shows a number of interesting alphabetic features: a probable bq construction; an R; an H; a definite i; a multi-levelled X, A and hinted

---

* for details of this trip, and later development of some of the ideas outlined tentatively in this commentary, see the author's 'Digging Up The Pas T in *Papers Delivered At The Symposium Of Linguistic Onto-Genetics (grOnk* Final Series #5. Toronto, 1985). ('Digging Up The Pas T' is PROBABLE SYSTEMS 36).

RAM■DA IN■ WINN

roads as energy accelerators + decelerators
(depending on direction you are travelling)

- early line H site
- it is felt the diagonal
- |—| elements were
  placed thus to
  yield at placement
  connecting with
  the Alex ■ pyramid.

i site (note
pyramid on
side to create
dot (•) on i

× ←16 WELLINGTON
AVE

bq ■ site →18

mapped
site →

Assiniboine   River

10 & 17 (as shown on map) are strange geomatic land
formations with dubious connections to alphabet
■■■■■ ■■■ ■■■■■■■■

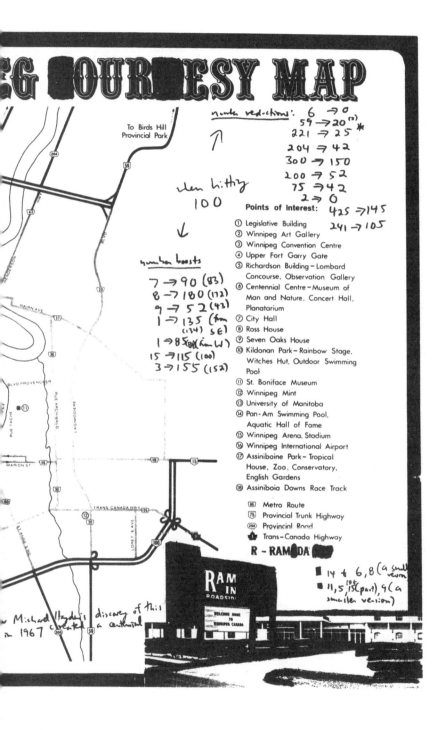

ЕG ЦОUR ЕSY MAP

To Birds Hill
Provincial Park

number reductions: 6 → 0
59 → 20 (?) *
221 → 25
204 → 42
300 → 150
200 → 52
75 → 42
2 → 0

when hitting
100

number boosts
7 → 90 (83)
8 → 180 (172)
9 → 52 (43)
1 → 135 (from (134) SE)
1 → 85 (ox from W)
15 → 115 (100)
3 → 155 (152)

Points of Interest: 425 → 145
241 → 105

① Legislative Building
② Winnipeg Art Gallery
③ Winnipeg Convention Centre
④ Upper Fort Garry Gate
⑤ Richardson Building – Lombard
    Concourse, Observation Gallery
⑥ Centennial Centre – Museum of
    Man and Nature, Concert Hall,
    Planatarium
⑦ City Hall
⑧ Ross House
⑨ Seven Oaks House
⑩ Kildonan Park – Rainbow Stage,
    Witches Hut, Outdoor Swimming
    Pool
⑪ St. Boniface Museum
⑫ Winnipeg Mint
⑬ University of Manitoba
⑭ Pan-Am Swimming Pool,
    Aquatic Hall of Fame
⑮ Winnipeg Arena, Stadium
⑯ Winnipeg International Airport
⑰ Assiniboine Park – Tropical
    House, Zoo, Conservatory,
    English Gardens
⑱ Assiniboia Downs Race Track

[85] Metro Route
[75] Provincial Trunk Highway
[204] Provincial Road
🍁 Trans-Canada Highway

R - RAM DA

■ 14 & 6,8 (a small
    version
■ 11, 5, 15 (part), 9 (a
    smaller version)

RAM IN
ROADSIDE

WELCOME HOME TO
WINNIPEG CANADA

w Michael Haydn's discovery of this
in 1967 created a centennial

at H site. Wildwood Park (with its various alphabetic sections) is located close to the R and is here labelled 'dreamed site.'

but the more important feature here is the energy grid within which these letters are contained. what this map points to is a whole pattern of energy paths, alphabetic routings within which messages are contained.* these routings (lost to the average eye amidst the welter of streets, but here, in this map i found, foregrounded) point to a larger link that the activity of reading creates, a link between the neuron pathways of the brain and the earth as a possible macro-mind in which human beings are simply complex thot nodes.** but this preliminary report seeks simply to present the information uncovered from the accompanying map (i have blacked out certain information to disguise the map's source since, as i have discovered to my chagrin, there are those who would wish to suppress this line of research even as there are others who wish to dismiss it thru ridicule).

SOME CALCULATIONS: TABLE 1 shows alphabetic values for a range of speeds from 1 to 312. TABLES 2&3 take a number of numbered energy routes and details them in terms of acceleration & deceleration.

Table 1: calculating accelerator & decelerator rates

A	B	C	D	E	F	G	H	I	J	K	L	M
1	2	3	4	5	6	7	8	9	10	11	12	13
27	28	29	30	31	32	33	34	35	36	37	38	39
53	54	55	56	57	58	59	60	61	62	63	64	65
79	80	81	82	83	84	85	86	87	88	89	90	91
105	106	107	108	109	110	111	112	113	114	115	116	117
131	132	133	134	135	136	137	138	139	140	141	142	143
157	158	159	160	161	162	163	164	165	166	167	168	169
183	184	185	186	187	188	189	190	191	192	193	194	195
209	210	211	212	213	214	215	216	217	218	219	220	221
235	236	237	238	239	240	241	242	243	244	245	246	247
261	262	263	264	265	266	267	268	269	270	271	272	273
287	288	289	290	291	292	293	294	295	296	297	298	299

* again, see the 'Digging Up the Pas T' article for an extensive commentary on the still mysterious Manitoba alphabet cult.
** as of the typing-up of this part of the final draft – August 14th, 1988 – these ideas are not yet worked out, but they will form the basis of a future PROBABLE SYSTEMS.

N	O	P	Q	R	S	T	U	V	W	X	Y	Z
14	15	16	17	18	19	20	21	22	23	24	25	26
40	41	42	43	44	45	46	47	48	49	50	51	52
66	67	68	69	70	71	72	73	74	75	76	77	78
92	93	94	95	96	97	98	99	100	101	102	103	104
118	119	120	121	122	123	124	125	126	127	128	129	130
144	145	146	147	148	149	150	151	152	153	154	155	156
170	171	172	173	174	175	176	177	178	179	180	181	182
196	197	198	199	200	201	202	203	204	205	206	207	208
222	223	224	225	226	227	228	229	230	231	232	233	234
248	249	250	251	252	253	254	255	256	257	258	259	260
274	275	276	277	278	279	280	281	282	283	284	285	286
300	301	302	303	304	305	306	307	308	309	310	311	312

N.B. – Accelerator and decelerator calculations are usually expressed as follows:

1A(1)

2A(27)

3A(53) & so on, tho they could be expressed simply as: 1A, 2A, 3A, etc. The value of each speed unit has not been finally determined but could be expressed fairly accurately as LPT (Letters Per Thot)

Table 2: some accelerator calculations

1G(7)	4L(90)
1H(8)	7X(180)
1I(9)	2Z(52)
1A(1) from SE	6E(135)
1 A(1) from W	4G(85)
1O(15)	5K(115)
1C(3)	6Y(155)

Table 3: some decelerator calculations

1F(6)	stops
3G(59)	1T(20)
9M(221)	1Y(25)
8V(204)	2P(42)
12N(300)	6T(150)
8R(200)	2Z(52)
3W(75)	2P(42)
1B(2)	stops
171(425)	60(145)
10G(241)	5A(105)

N.B. 4V(100) and 4W(101) chart the course of a major energy interface that almost encloses the rest of the grid. most routes go through deceleration or acceleration when they hit it. 9M(221) passes straight through the energy interface without changing speed, but decelerates at intersection with 4L(90). the reason for this remains unexplained tho a workable theory designates 9M(221) as the main entry point for all particles first entering the grid.

IMPLICATIONS:

On the map, I (the mirror of H –
tho here, admittedly, in lower case)
precedes H (&, by implication, & in terms
of the discovery made in 'commentary 1') its twin S*

S is the disguised 8
H is the disguised ⊟
both lie eight places in from
their edge of the alphabet

The completed formulation then would be:

I H S R **

Since I, H & R are located on the map as actual sites, we may assume that S exists as one of the other sites. Most likely (in my opinion) is ⑮ where four modified S shapes overlap — i.e.

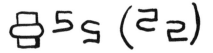

---

* precedes because it lies North of, on the map. North/South alignments are not yet fully understood but they do appear to have been crucial to the alphabet cult.
** note that the IHS in 'commentary 1' was an intuitive leap but forms the justification for the search for the S on the found map. it is interesting to speculate the route this three letter cluster has travelled from the early alphabet cult to finally end up as a Christian monogram, but it is most likely another instance (as with the Christmas tree etc.) of Christianity adapting itself to an earlier tradition in order to be more easily accepted.

(One is reminded of ⑱, the bq site, also located near a ■ sign. This makes it reasonable to assume that other overlap figures once existed at ⑭ ⑪ ⑤ & ⑨ .)*

Using, then, ⑮ as the probable S location,
we can arrive at the following:

S	⑮	lies on	4L(90)
R	⑬	lies on	2P(42)
H	①	lies on	3J(62)
I	⑦	lies on	2Z(52)

Looking at the map it is obvious that:

S decelerates to R (90 to 85 to 62 to 42);
I can only reach H by first accelerating (42 to 85)
& then decelerating (85 to 62);
H reaches I the same way (62 to 85 to 42);
R accelerates to S (42 to 62 to 85 to 90).

Similarly
S decelerates to reach I & H:
I is constant to R but accelerates to S;
R is constant to I but accelerates to H;
H decelerates to R & accelerates to S.

If following the alphabetic sequence then, as in a cult worship ceremony, the rates would be as follows:

from H start at 3J and accelerate to 4G and then decelerate to 2P;
from I maintain a constant rate of 2P to R;
from R continue at 2P, then accelerate to 3J, then to 4G & then
up to 4L (top LPT rate on this circuit);
from S continue at 4L then decelerate to 4G and then to 3J for
the return to H.

---

* given the geomantic capabilities of the alphabet cult it is worth pointing out here the S's in the shapes of both the Red River and the aSSiniboine. (note, too, the R & S presence in the river naming.)

A reading of HIRS*, as in any reading, involves both acceleration & deceleration i.e. i do not read at one continuous tempo. There are peaks and valleys, areas of text where i move quickly and areas where i move more slowly (the classic 'skip-over-the-description' pattern of the average reader is a typical example of one manifestation of this.

---

* PROBABLE SYSTEMS 30: It should be noted here that the alphabetic relationships of H I R S to the larger issue of gender in language is not accidental. If we read HIRS as a contraction of HI[(S) & (HE)]RS (and note how SHE is the contracted element) then we realize that here R is the feminizer (cf. *The Martyrology Bk 4*).

HE & S̲HE

HIM & HE̲R

HI̲S & HE̲RS

if in HERS, S is the possessive

then in SHE does S possess the HE?

i.e. are these simply fragmentary inscriptions?

viz:

[ ]'s HE

which as a fragment would seem to point back to a
deeper rooted matriarchal society.

[ ]('S?)HER

[ ]('S?)HER'S

Or similarly:

MAN

WO   MAN

could be the suppressed

WO'S   MAN

this sense (the mother/woman possesses the man) was later
buried & (in fact) turned around and WOMAN came to be
seen as a possession of MAN.

but who then is WO?

cf. WODEN as in WO'S DEN (i.e. the place where WO lives).
WO'S MAN lives in WO'S DEN (with its notion of WOmb,etc.), was later
translated into ODIN as the father figure. the mother disappeared – suppressed.

we could reconstruct the missing fragments as:

[WO]'S HE

[WO]('S?) HER

& [WO]('S?) HER'S

But what is pointed to here is the ability to analyze reading at a finer level of detail i.e. the change of tempo from letter to letter in any cluster of letters (be they words or more abstract groupings). What this map gives us access to is an understanding of 'the speed of thot,' a still dimly understood notion which, we can see, was once outered in the now forgotten &/or suppressed rituals and traditions of the Manitoba alphabet cult.

With the limited resources available to me, i have not yet been able to free the time necessary to examine the other letter sites indicated on the map.* some preliminary, & highly tentative, exploration suggests the possibility that ⑩ & ⑰ represent areas where earth was removed to help in the shaping of alphabetic signs at other locations (tho why they would choose sites so near the energy interface remains puzzling – perhaps nearness to the river, and the ability therefore to float materials needed on rafts, was one of the major criteria for all these sites.) note that ⑰ lies on a major deceleration route & ⑩ on a major acceleration route.

Were decelerating & accelerating units joined together to energize and create a balance of forces in the megalithic alphabet works? i.e. is the concept 'speed-of-thot' related to the concept of a balanced mind? was that worked with, sought after, in some way, pre-historically? is the notion of yin/yang (its relationship to the idea of geomancy) a

---

in *The Martyrology Bk 4* we saw the S was the feminizer that birthed the I in IS. similarly here, when we recover the lost fragment, we begin to under-stand the S as part of the understood phrase:

HE [i]S [out of (or birthed) by] WO

there is a sense here too of WOE & suffering & of a woman's period (syntactical pun?) being referred to as a curse (because it is a reminder of WO'S DEN? i.e. a now suppressed tradition).

WO, and other lost goddesses and gods celebrated in the traditions of the Manitoba alphabet cult, will be gone into in more detail in subsequent PROBABLE SYSTEMS.

written: February 10th, 1978.
additional research and final draft – August 16th, 1988.

*still true as of August 16th, 1988.

trace of that earlier process? do these Winnipeg letter sites (15 in all, with a possible 16th) represent points of alphabetic balance & were they sacred from both a written and spoken point of view? The questions multiply. Some answers seem to emerge. Others merge or seem to elude us. But not forever.

written: 1973 & 1978
additional research and final draft: August 1988

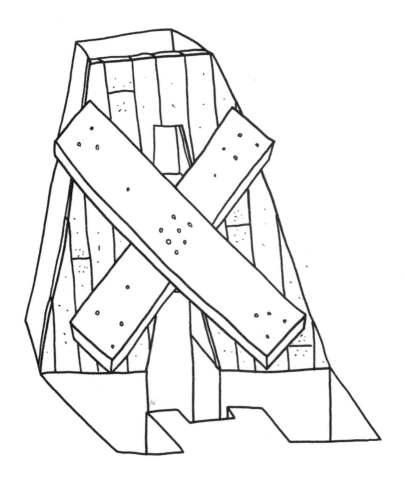

The Frog Variations

for Louise Prael

1   Dawn   fog
                          log
                          bog

      Noon   frog
                          log
                          bog

      Dusk   fog
                          frog
                          bog

2   fog fog fog frog fog

3   moonfrog
       pondfrog
       frogfrog

4   (definition of a lily-pad)
                  fragile
                  frog île

5   (the frog's obsession with the fly)
                  frog'll oggle all

6   frog's tongue: fly catcher
       frog's eye: bird measure
       frog stung
       frog sigh
                bird fly

7   o moon
    no moon

     o frog
    no frog

     o pond
    no pond

     o
    no

     o
    no

     o
    no

8 splash

  splayed beneath the bending ash
  fragile children of the great bog
  frog

  pond

  poised under the autumn frond
  more singers of the dark water croon
  moon

9 into the sky at night
  the moon & all her frogs drop

  under the brilliant light of the pond
  rippling life goes on

bpNichol
July 10th, 1981
'one of the Basho Street Kids'

dreamed anthology 2

a poem by bill bissett

                    deer in the forest
            between   the trees
            where i   sense them
                the traces   their hooves leave
                in the wet earth
                        wet
                day   i cannot
                    remember
            the way   they
            used to   move
            then   when
                i was
                younger

                younger
            days
        the hunger
                returns
            the dry   reds
        the nights   the sky
                burned

                *   *   *   *   *
                    *   *   *   *   *
        *   *   *   *   *   *   *
            *   *   *   *   *   *
                *   *   *   *   *

                    along the highway
            starry
                        night
            the white
                        line
                burns
                        the eyes
                    deer
                        crossing
        where the mind
                        moves

                    (
                    ( )   )
            (   )   )
                (   )

                                    goodnight
                    the mountains
                                    mass against the sky
                like clouds
                            peaks
                                invisible
                    where the deer roam
                                    proud and
                        wild

                                    – entire poem
                                    UNTITLED:

                                    January 17th, 1967

Three Months in New York City

The Actual Life of Language 1

CARTER

FIRE
SNOW

MINERS
CARTER
QUEENS

COURT
UNIONS

BEGIN ISRAELI ISRAELIS KIDNAP OK

BARE

ISRAEL
PEACE
FEAR
DRIVE

ISRAELI

BEGIN
STEEL
CARTER
4

ARRAIGN
STRIKE
REPORT
'BUNNIES'
NURSING

COP
SCHOOL
HOLD
'DEAD'
LOCAL
HINT

HOW WALL SENATE TRACE SENATE SPINKS

EX-DRUG SAM I FORT 51 PROBE

2
BOOK
KIDNAPED
SUN
2
BERKOWITZ

OIL
SON
MORO
AGREE
CARTER

HEAVY
PATTY
ORDER
RESCUE
LBJ

SICK BERKOWITZ JOE HUNT CARTER PORT

RIDERS MUST A

dreamed anthology 3

a text by Sheila Watson

I start out with the idea of place to fix you
there, Mommy. Interwoven. Interspecies.

— a fragment only

from 'Six Unanswered Questions After Michael Anthin'

March 1979

Sixteen Lilypads

frog	fro?	fr?g	?rog
f?og	?r?g	??og	f?o?
?ro?	fr??	f??g	???g
f???	??o?	?r??	????

dreamed anthology 4

a poem by Michael Ondaatje

> *tiny in the high wind a feather*
> > *flung in the air and*

out

– entire poem
UNTITLED:

April 9th, 1979

---

in my dream he also tells me about another poem he is working on, all about a trip to Ceylon, which is titled 'The Green Bear.'

prayer

teach me song. i
would sing. teach me
love. i would
i were open
to it. teach me
to pray
privately, praise
quietly
those things
i should. show me
the grace
of movement
& touch – that much
i would offer
to her. teach me
more – a way
for me
to reach her
who beckons
hesitantly. teach me
to be sure.

Sketching 1

David Phillips reading January 31st, 1981

1

the poems on the table
cigarettes
the beer

voice is
clearly articulated

all the mind gathers

a life

the

here

2

'blue hydrangea'

the colour of air

a cat's name
the same
referred to

feline in the err
or moment

blue as
this ink this
pen

only a memory when
the poem's typed or
printed

3

'i/you'

'we' to us
'them'

him & her

or
  , hey,
they

4

fast words

lines

all the sketches catch is
or as

        (just long enough to
let the words sink in

(to the skin

to the bottom of the sea

(ear as channel
to the mind
(did i time that right?)

)right)

)right)

5

drink the beer

smoke

the cigarette

goes in &
what comes out is

poems

> o 'em's the thing
> o 'em's the song
> o 'em's the one
> all night long

-etry

6

just the slightest shift'll
shif the thing

no longer where we thot it was
what we thot it was

a little loop returns to

the view from the window
(that line in a poem
(the tone of a single voice
reading)
words written)
other times ago

7

get it right

it ends

a lifetime pursuit

hope against the real odds
it continues in you's
over   on

formula for determining reader's ability to gain access to the book/machine

$$100 \left(\frac{10}{P(C)} \right) = A$$

where P represents the degree of adherence to, or antipathy towards, traditional book/machine values on the part of the reader.*

where C represents the degree to which the book/machine is utilized traditionally or in a non-traditional way by the writer?**

where A represents the reader's ability to gain access to the book/machine

in using the above formula: where $\frac{10}{P(C)}$ > **1** read as 1.

EXAMPLES

1) Fred (a traditionalist rated 10 on the P scale) reads the latest Arthur Hailey novel (rating of 1 on the C scale).

computation

$100 \left(\frac{10}{P(C)} \right) = A$

$100 \left(\frac{10}{10(1)} \right) = 100 \left(\frac{10}{10} \right) = 100 \left(\frac{1}{1} \right)$

$= 100$

A = 100% access for Fred to Arthur Hailey's novel.

2) Fred picks up Madeline Gins' *WORD RAIN* (8.5 on the C scale).

---

* P is rated on a scale of 1 to 10, where 1 represents complete antipathy towards, & 10 complete acceptance of, traditional book/machine values.
** C is rated on a scale of 1 to 10, where 1 represents traditional utilization of the book/machine & 10 a radical departure from, or extreme change in the utilization.

computation

$$100 \left(\frac{10}{10(8.5)} \right) = 100 \left(\frac{10}{85} \right) = 100 \left(\frac{2}{17} \right) = \frac{200}{17}$$

$$= 11.8$$

11.8% access for Fred to *WORD RAIN*.

3) Angela (a radical reader rated 1 on the P scale) picks up the latest Arthur Hailey novel after Fred recommends it to her.

computation

since $\frac{10}{P(C)} = \frac{10}{1}$ & is, therefore, > 1 we read it as 1

$$100(1)$$
$$= 100$$

100% access for Angela to Arthur Hailey's novel.

4) Angela decides to try Madeline Gins' *WORD RAIN*, even tho Fred didn't like it.

computation

since $\frac{10}{1(8.5)} = 1.2$ & is, therefore, > 1 we read it as 1

$$100(1)$$
$$= 100$$

100% access for Angela to Madeline Gins' *WORD RAIN*.

5) Mickey (rated 5 on the P scale) picks up *WORD RAIN* at Angela's recommendation.

computation

$$100 \left(\frac{10}{5(8.5)} \right) = 100 \left(\frac{10}{42.5} \right) = \frac{1000}{42.5} = 23.5$$

23.5% access for Mickey to *WORD RAIN*.

i've included only a handful of examples here, enough to demonstrate that the conclusions reached by the application of this formula are consistent with traditional assumptions about readers, a person with a rating of 1 on the P scale would have equal access to both Arthur Hailey's latest novel and Madeline Gins' *WORD RAIN*, whereas a person with a rating of 10 would have no trouble with the Hailey novel but would be unable to gain access to the Gins one. in short: the results favour an Angela over either a Fred or a Mickey.

it should be noted that greater accuracy could be achieved by basing the ratings on a 1 to 1000 scale (depending on how many readers &/or writers are under consideration). in time an independent body could be established to rate all the novels ever published, tho some allowance for historical shifts in reading patterns, comprehension across language changes, etc., would have to be factored into the formula for that to be feasible.

written: 1973/74
revised version: August 27th, 1988

dreamed anthology 5

a poem by Childe Roland

SO I REPORT YOU SAID NO TO THIS
I REPORT YOU SAID NO TO THIS
REPORT YOU SAID NO TO THIS
YOU SAID NO TO THIS
SAID NO TO THIS
NO TO THIS
TO THIS
THIS

— entire poem
title: 'So I Report You Said No To This'

October 1986

Interrupted Nap

a verbal/pre-verbal landscape

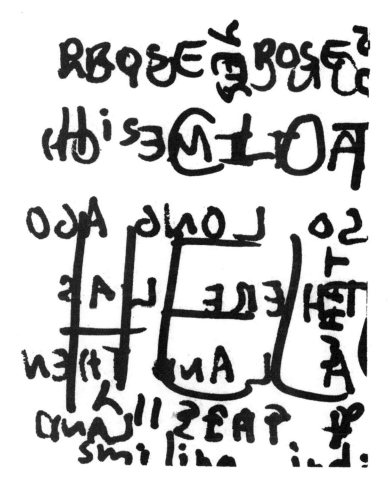

ONCE UPON

A TIME OH

SO, LONG AGO

THERE WAS

A LAND THEN

LAND

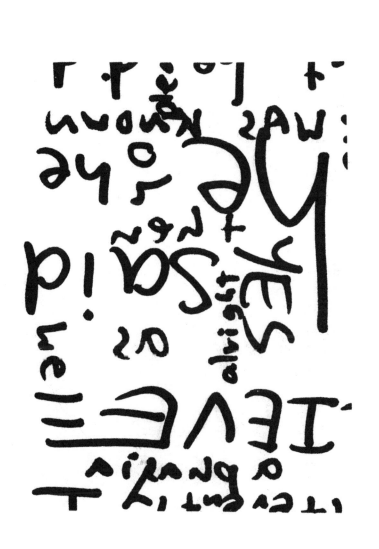

WAS KNOWN

ONG

then

bias

as

aphasia

SAYS

please

IT Now

OH HE

HE removes this and

WAS KNOWN

this

break

THE

how t

this bad

WAS KNOWN

First Snow – Dawn

all that weight on that branch
waiting

Castlegar
March 12th, 1980

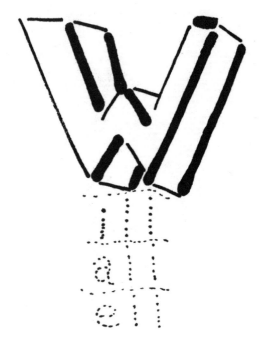

Kite 2
October 1971

```
        asea ease  ease
        ease seas  seas
        seas asea  asea
       asea ease  ease
       ease seas  seas
      seas asea  asea
      easease ease
       aseas  seas
       aseas asea
      easeasease
      seas aseas
     asea  aseas
     ease  easease
    seas  seas asea
   asea      ease seas
   ease      asea ease
 seas       seas asea
  ease        ease seas
  asea        seas  ease
   seas       asea     asea
    ease ease       seas
    aseaseas          ease
     seasea           seas
      ease            asea
      as             ease
                     seas
                     asea
                    ease
```

Ludwig Wittgenstein & DADA
(an historical footnote)

BROWN BOOK 33)

Ludwig Wittgenstein gives as an example the sentence 'aacaddd' in which the letters are equated with arrows which are understood as movements carried out by the person comprehending the sentence according to the following chart:

a	←
b	→
c	↑
d	↓

we can construct two other sentences & graph their movements:

a) sentence: CADA ↑→↓→

b) sentence: DADA ↓→↓→

BROWN BOOK 34)

The order 'CADA' generates the ornamental linear design

if 33) is applied to 34) the actual sentence generated in 34 can be read as CADACADACADA where 'CADA' as an order is the understood sentence CADACADACADA.

if the system Wittgenstein proposed in 34) is applied to our second sentence DADA (generated by Wittgenstein's system in 33) then 'DADA' as an order generates the ornamental linear design

(note the
'staircase' phenomenon.)
           In western languages the print page leads us deeper into meaning from top left to bottom right. Wittgenstein in his *Brown Book* 34) system generates the actual graphing of DADA if we understand it as an order to move deeper into language. The fact that any staircase goes both up & down indicates that 'DADA' as a sentence could be translated to read 'move deeper into language by which i mean allow yourself to move back & forth freely thru all levels of language.'

bpNichol
February 14th, 1974

Negatives 1: Force Movements

(for & after Nelson Ball)

automobile poem

The sound of
   sting

grass poems

the place

   – for William Roberts,
   a painter
you see a disturbance of the grass
see a disturbance of the grass do
a disturbance of the grass do you
disturbance of the grass do you see
turbance of the grass do you see a
ance of the grass do you see a dis
of the grass do you see a disturb
the grass do you see a disturbance
grass do you see a disturbance of
   a mouse or a house was? do you see a dis-
      turbance of the
mouse or a house was? (where
or a house was? (where a
a house was? (where a mouse
house was? (where a mouse or
was? (where a mouse or a
? (where a mouse or a house
(where a mouse or a house was

bird poem

. Or looks up at
the title of
this poem.

                    sea poem

& you read into that a meaning.

                    train poem

I hear:

& it is

                    fall

This poem occurs because
                    ing words

         this page.

         bridge poem

It is
         by the press of girders

but a

sends the
brain
crashing.

            highway poem

Up ahead
            in
the mind

dreamed anthology 6

a poem by Luella Booth Kerr

    Behind the Empress Hotel

    beyond the number of leaves – tree

    beyond the number of windows – me

– entire poem
title: 'Behind The Empress Hotel'

November 19th, 1986

Sketching 2

CCMC with Steve McCaffery

1

an empty stage

a place in which there is nothing
there are objects

no objections

a beginning

2

birds

this is an abstraction

this is traction when
the finger slips
tips

mouth music muses

chooses
           which is not a ryme

time's abandoned for a tone
a kind of random tune
moves the meant

3

saxophony

symphony

synthesizerphony

guitarphony

'do the pony phony'

4

screaming or a kind of pleading

is there a value
judgement is there

simply speaking simply

chordial
musical

broadway

5

voices / ices / o
ver
    / er
       /
          hmmm

an observation in the midst of
not / sing / ing

'in the human head'

walking the bass line

/ home /

6

two beats

two drums

two cheeks
pounded

im

     er again

WILLED

7

auto horn
auto harp
auto heart

YELLING

siren
sighing wren
weep willed

BIRDLAND

8

quarreltet

argumental

so the brain in brain is
mainly in the plain telling

or a sea
washes over me

sound wave

9

altoed states

his attack jack is back to basics
cohere to there

to & fro in the world &
struck sure

flim flamenco densities

u's
    v's

y z

Music Gallery
Toronto, February 24th, 1981

deathad death'shead

I

tor	nado	
tor	nato	
tor	nata	1
tor	nada	
tor	nado	

II

ca	nada	
ca	nado	
ca	nato	
ca	nata	1
ca	nada	

III

tor	ca	nada	
tor	ca	nado	
tor	ca	nato	
tor	ca	nata	1
tor	ca	nada	

IV

ca	tor	nado	
ca	tor	nato	
ca	tor	nata	1
ca	tor	nada	
ca	tor	nado	

V

```
      tor
N  A  D  O
      ca
N  A  D  A
```

based on an Advertisement in the *Globe & Mail* 1978 for a PANAVIA
TORNADO placed by the company to influence purchase for NATO.

Remembrance

The Actual Life of Language 2

GAS
Sooner..
8-4!
The
Iran
We
Mississauga

2

Inferno

3

UIC

Sun

ATKEY'S

4

Iran

Crossing

Egypt

5

D-Day

Joe

HALF-FORGOTTEN

Honoring

6

7

Sewell

AFTER

9

10

Remembrance

11

Oh,

A

All

Toronto Sun
November 11th, 1979

catching frogs

for LeRoy Gorman

jar din

---
sea
light
sky

---
sky
light
sea

---
light
sea
light

---
light
sky
light

---
light
light
light

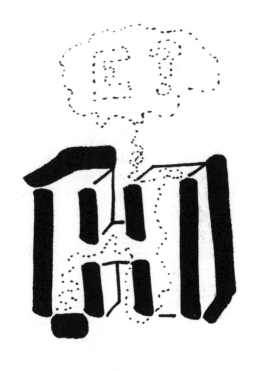

Kite 3 (dream)
for Steve October 1971

Cree Song

for Gus

a e o ah
o o o o
ah e
ah a
    ah o
      o ah
ah ah ah ah
ah o e a

                bay bee bo bah
                bo bo bo bo
                bah bee
                bah bay
                      bah bo
                      bo bah
                bah bah bah bah
                bah bo bee bay

a bee o bah
o bo o bo
ah bee
bah bay
    ah bo
      o bah
ah bah ah bah
ah bo e bay

1965

translation (a continuation of PS 11)

In Probable Systems 11* I constructed a table of alphabetic bases. In the process a number of questions were raised which this system will attempt to deal with. To re-cap briefly: the existing alphabet (if considered in numerical terms) is base 27 or, as I prefer to call it, base alphabet; to achieve the concept 'alphabet' (now revealed to be the name of the next letter beyond Z**) we must write it thus — a@ — where @ denotes the empty place (& thus the letter after a@ would have to be written aa, the next letter ab, & so on). Now having constructed such a table the possibility of translating texts into other bases instantly emerges. That is what this system proposes to examine.

Let us use as an example Rene Daumal's 1938 poem 'Originie de l'Astronomie'. We will take the first line and use two different approaches in our translating of it:

1) translate it into a different base
2) consider each word as the complex expression
   of a single letter

Before proceeding further a word of explanation is in order. In base alphabet the first seven places have the following numerical values (expressed in base 10, of course):

387,420,489	14,348,907	531,441	19,683	729	27	1
		G	R	E	A	T
			D	O	G	S
			B	A	R	K
	L	O	U	D	L	Y

---

* See the author's *Zygal*.
** This is the last point at which the names of any of these letters beyond Z is clear. It is certainly possible that each of the letters beyond Z has its special name, and certainly certain arcane schools of mysticism suggest this. But if so that information has been lost, unless we follow some kind of 'lost culture in a lost valley' pipedream.

Using the nonsense phrase, 'Great dogs bark loudly,' we can illustrate what is meant by the notion of a single word being the complex expression of a single letter. The 'G' in 'Great,' for instance, in numerical terms would be expressed as 7 (its place in the alphabet) x 531,441 (the position it occupies in base alphabet). To continue, the 'R' would be expressed as 18 x 19,683. And so on. In order to do the translation which follows it is first necessary then to translate the letters out of the particular bases they are in, into their numerical equivalents (numerical base 10). I show you one such operation in order to make the mechanics of this method of translation clear.

Multiplying the place value of the letter (in the alphabet) times the value of the place it occupies in base alphabet, we arrive at the following answers:

$$
\begin{array}{rcl}
G\ [7] \times 531{,}441 & = & 3720087 \\
R\ [18] \times 19{,}683 & = & 354294 \\
E\ [5] \times 729 & = & 3645 \\
A\ [1] \times 27 & = & 27 \\
T\ [20] \times 1 & = & 20 \\
\hline
\text{GREAT} & = & 4078073 \quad \text{(numerical base 10)}
\end{array}
$$

To translate GREAT into another base we simply make a series of divisions by the value of the equivalent places in the base we are translating into. For example, if we were translating GREAT into base J (the easiest base to translate into since its numerical equivalent is 10*) the computations would go as follows**:

$$
\begin{array}{rcl}
1000000/\underline{4078073} & = & 4 \\
\quad\ \ 4000000 & & \\
100000/\underline{078073} & = & 0 \\
\quad\ \ 000000 & &
\end{array}
$$

---

* I would remind the reader at this point that place values in base 10 are all multiples of 10 (i.e. the units, tens, hundreds, thousands, ten-thousands, hundred-thousands, millions, etc.) even as in base alphabet the place values are all multiples of 27 (i.e. units, twenty-sevenths, seven hundred and twenty nines, nineteen thousand six hundred & eighty-threes, etc.)

** I recognize that this is totally unnecessary but such painstaking detail at this point helps to illustrate the actual translation process for those who may wish to translate from base alphabet (numerical equivalent 27) into base M (numerical equivalent 13) an obviously more complicated problem.

$$10000/\underline{78}073 = 7$$
$$\underline{70000}$$
$$1000/\underline{8}073 = 8$$
$$\underline{8000}$$
$$100/073 = 0$$
$$\underline{000}$$
$$10/\underline{7}3 = 7$$
$$\underline{70}$$
$$1/\underline{3} = 3$$
$$\underline{3}$$

Next we translate the numerical equivalents arrived at back into their alphabetic equivalents*:

$$4078073 = D@GH@GC**$$

In adapting the system illustrated here to a different base simply begin your division with the first place numerical equivalent lower in value than the concept you are dividing into. For example, in base V (a base we'll be using in a moment) the first division would be

$$234567/\underline{4078073}$$

where 234567 is the value of the 5th place in base V.

Let us now apply what we have learned to the first line of 'Originie de l'Astonomie' –

'Le son du soleil dans ton coeur'

The first thing that strikes us about this line is that it could be the expression of a concept in any base from base V (the largest letter in the line being U) to one well beyond base alphabet. For the sake of this particular translation we will consider the line to have been written in base V*** and will translate the line from base V thru base alphabet into base J. Using the method previously illustrated the first set of translations generate the following line in base alphabet:

---

* Obviously base J has a limited palette (or, indeed, palate) of letters – A thru I.
** How to pronounce '@' remains a problem.
*** In fact a close reading of the poem reveals the word 'douze' in the 9th line thus fixing the piece as having been written in base alphabet. But because of

'Iz mbi da gbbyp@ benn mtg apzba'

The second set of translations (into base J) generate the following line:

'Bfi ied@ a@i abdfdebad ech@c a@@bd a@fad@h'

But we talked about also translating the line into a single word by considering each word in the original line as being the complex expression of a single letter. Thus in this line from Daumal, which I have taken as being written in base V, we have the 269th letter, followed by the 9540th letter, followed by the 109th letter, followed by the 124,645,214th letter, followed by the 53,083rd letter, followed by the 10,024th letter, followed, finally, by 1,061,408th letter. As can be seen the application of this particular system raises a number of fascinating conceptual problems not the least of which is the comprehension of a letter 124,645,213 letters beyond A. Seuss's *On Beyond Zebra* becomes a reality. The alphabet (a closed system) is opened up to the discovery of letters beyond Z. Since containing an infinite number of signs within the mind appears to be an impossibility, the majority of concepts are expressed as a combination of 26 basic signs* But why 26? The very concept of base alphabet makes us aware of the existence of other signs, of a larger set of possibilities, even as the concept of base J itself we were to replace '@' (the sign for the empty place) with 'O' (which is not used in the limited ten character set), we would generate the following translation of Daumal's line:

'Bfi iedo aoi abdfdebad echoc aoobd aofadoh'

This one simple step increases the vowels available to us in base J to four. Then by the broader application of base J we could rapidly decrease the number of excess words and increase the measurable nuance in the differentiation between the degrees of things thru, for instance, the increase of duration, etc. One way this might work could be:

---

the theoretical nature of our work in any case we will simply use this as a demonstration of certain paradoxes within the language.#

The above footnote was written circa 1974. Revising and retyping this piece now (November 1986) I find a certain je-jeune enthusiasm in many of my pronouncements that are difficult to edit out but should be noted.
* I am talking here about the arabic alphabet and the languages that make use of it. There is obviously room here for a fascinating study of comparative alphabetics and the position of the various letters in relation to each other in the larger alphabet to which our second translation system points.

IF: GREAT = DOGHOGC
THEN: GREATER = DOGHOGCC
AND: GREATEST = DOGHOGCCC

Since the ten letter code could, in fact, be any ten letters (I've rather arbitrarily chosen the first nine letters and then interpolated O), an optimum sound maximum flexibility code could be worked out.

However, the very act of considering words as complex expressions of single letters leads us to reconsider the nature of the sentence or, in this case, the line. Applying this system to the opening line of Daumal's 'Originie de l'Astronomie' we generated a word composed of a sequence of unwritable letters (letters for which there is no known sign*). But what happens if we then take the generated word and consider it as the complex expression of an even higher letter? We are forced to once again assign an arbitrary base to the word we have made from Daumal's line**. But giving it the assigned base value of the 2,000,000th letter (which is to say 'base 2,0000,000th letter') we arrive, thru translation, at:

the 17,216,305,280,002,741,161,712,212,332,020,049, 069,407th letter beyond A

---

* The concept of things which cannot be signed, letters which we can point to but cannot write down, points to the existence of worlds and knowledge that we have no way of expressing. At least here, in Probable Systems 22, we begin to find a way to chart some of that writing, even if the charted portions remain, finally, untranslatable into base alphabet.#

  # I am pointing here to the possibility that the very act of translating them into base alphabet garbles the message. We become caught up in *our* meaning and miss *their* meaning. See here how I point to *them* but am unable to say what it is I am signing. Is there some connection then between this activity and what happens when I 'forget to sign a letter? discover an unsigned note? etc.?

** The arbitrariness of these values remains problematic in terms of any actual 'proof' or, indeed, of arriving at a definitive reading of any particular work of literature in terms of what I go on to propose in this paragraph. Clearly our standard base in most western languages is base alphabet. This is well established by historical usage. And the very notion of a base A, a base B, a base C, etc., points to the fact that certain configurations of letters have different meanings depending on the base we read them in. The word 'bee' is a perfect example of the problem any translator faces who lacks a well-established key to what base the text under consideration is written in.

By extension, then, we could, by considering the sequence of sentences which compose stanzas or paragraphs, generate even more difficult to conceive letters, arriving at, finally, a point where, for instance, a novel like Proust's *Remembrance of Things Past* could be considered as simply the complex expression of a single letter an unimaginable distance beyond A. There is certainly a sense in which any novel or poem is nothing more than one complex operating sign and, indeed, looking at works of literature in such a way gives us fresh access to such obviously complex works as Victor Coleman's *America*.

Those of you who have followed my researches will recall that in an earlier Probable System I referred to the concept of nearest whole letter. In *America* Coleman appears to be using the double acrostic form, beginning each line with (in sequence) the letters from the words QUEEN OF CUPS, KING OF CUPS, etc., so that the left and right hand margins of the poems spell out the same words:

Question: Political? Iraq

U	u
E	e
E	e
N	n
O	o
F	f
C	c
U	u
P	p
S	s

But it is my contention that what Coleman has really done in these poems is to enter the microcosm of our ordinary base alphabet world. Looking at the first line of QUEEN OF CUPS we see how he has charted what lies between the 'Q' and the 'q,' which is to say what lies within the letter, its component parts. In doing so he points the way towards a vast new galaxy of previously unrecognized signs. Starting from the minimal operating signs of writing, the letters, he moves outward (inward) into whole poems, a whole sequence of poems, and in the process begins to chart a universe, lettrism carried forward into the main body of poetry.

In considering these two systems of translation then we have been forced to look at writing in a totally new way. In doing so we begin to gain some clues as to the possible origin of language. One thing that is immediately obvious is that such a way of looking at language points towards a return to one tongue. What is the difference in the translation systems proposed between french, english and spanish? There is none. The words of these languages are simply different signs from the same continuum. We begin to understand then that the breakup of the one mother tongue (the pre babel state) also meant a breakup of the Ur-alphabet (or urphabet as it is more commonly referred to), a reduction of signs, a possible loss of intelligence, the trading in of a much more complex system of operating signs for a more portable alphabet*. At this same time the concept of the empty place disappeared from common linguistic usage**, and the language tribes choosing to work with the signs comprising what we call the arabian alphabet also claimed certain combinations of those signs as their own. Why each tribal language found that necessary is not known and is, in any case, beyond the scope of this particular system, this essay.

written: 1971–74
additional research & final draft: November 1986

---

* See my earlier (1972) 'Probable Systems 14: Rediscovery of the 22 letter alphabet — An Archaeological Report' in *Canadian ''Pataphysics* (Underwhich Editions, 1981) for a detailed take on this. I would mention that more recent researches (1986) suggest that at the time of the breakup of the urphabet a process of conscious choosing was in operation, that the realphabet posited in PS14 represents the original choices of the urelders and that our current alphabet emerged out of that. Needless to say all this throws the problem of translation into even deeper confusion. I would add, too, that the alphabet cult# was long forgotten at the time of the urphabet breakup.

   # See my later (1981) 'Probably Systems 36: Digging Up the Pas T' in *Papers De-livered At The Symposium Of Linguistic Onto-Genetics (grOnk* Final Series #5, 1985) for a detailed discussion of this cult and its influence on all subsequent language developments.

** There are some arguments now that the spaces between 'words' are nothing more than the empty place being signed in the only way it is possible to sign it — with nothing.

fr
pond
glop

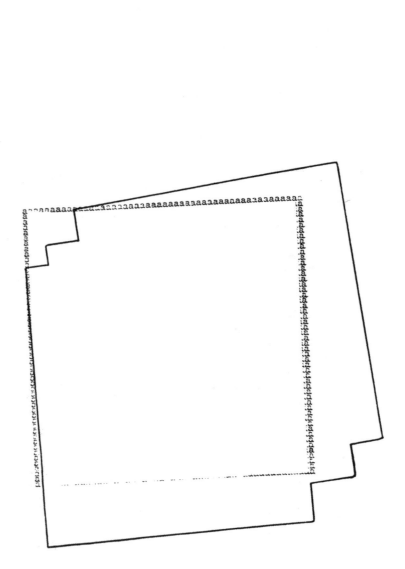

version bpN
of Clement Padin's *Tema y Variaciones*
(poema – proceso September 1972)
executed June 1973

If we regard a text as being the complex expression of a single letter (see Probable Systems 22), then what letter is 'Translating Apollinaire'* the complex expression of?

Let us examine one word from the text to establish the model to be used.

Nine letter places are contained in the word 'mountains.' Considered in base 10 terms then, the model for 'mountains' would be 100,000,000 i.e.

---

* 'Translating Apollinaire' was the author's first published poem (Blew Ointment, Vancouver, 1964). Written in 1963 in Toronto, the poem forms the basis for a research project entitled *Translating Translating Apollinaire* (two volumes published so far — Membrane Press, Milwaukee, 1979 & 1980). for the benefit of readers who may not have seen those volumes, the complete text of 'Translating Apollinaire' is included below:

Icharrus   winging up
Simon the Magician   from Judea   high in a tree
everyone   reaching for the sun
                    great towers of stone
built by the Aztecs, tearing their hearts out
to offer them, wet and beating

                    mountains,
cold wind, Machu Picchu hiding in the sun
unfound for centuries

cars whizzing by, sun
thru trees passing, a dozen
new wave films, flickering
on drivers' glasses

flat on their backs in the grass
a dozen bodies slowing turning brown

sun glares off the pages, 'soleil
cou coupé,' rolls in my window
flat on my back on the floor
becoming aware of it
for an instant

$$\frac{\text{mou,nta,ins}}{100,000,000}$$

But as already established in PS 11, 'Translating Apollinaire' is actually written in base alphabet (i.e. base 27) and thus the 'm' in mountains would have an equivalence of 13 in the 9th place in base alphabet, the 'o' an equivalence of 15 in the 8th place, the 'u' an equivalence of 21 in the 7th place, and so on. In order to understand which letter beyond A the entire text is a complex expression of then, it is necessary for the entire text to be translated out of base alphabet into base 10. Those wishing to examine the computations involved are welcome to visit the author at the Institute for Alphabet Archaeology in Toronto, Canada, and examine the records kept there. I will not bore you by including them here.

After translating all the words in the text from base alphabet into base 10 and totalling them, it was discovered that:

'Translating Apollinaire' is the complex expression of a single letter 54,786,210,294,570 letters beyond A.

original calculations: November 24th thru 26th, 1976
text written: November 1986

erotikon

for dick higgins

1) arrow

→

tick

⇁

2) e row

E E E

tack

⊢ ⊢ ⊢

3) a row

A A A A A A A A A A A A A A A A A A A A A A A A A A A

talk

... anyone at all. Allan ably assisted Alex's attempts at articulating an arguably apoetic approach. 'After all,' Alex argued, 'adjectives are applicable and allow amazingly amusing afterthoughts.' Allan, admittedly angry, acclaimed Alex's argument. 'Absolutely,' avowed Allan. Ann, ambiguous, avoided Alex and Allan and addressed Arnold, an amateur archaeologist attending an arts academy at Athens. 'Aren't adjectives anti-absolute?' asked Ann. Arnold, amused, attacked Ann's attempted alliance: 'Assinine!' Ann, appropriately annoyed, asked Allan's assistance. Allan avoided Ann's appeal. 'Aren't all arguments?' asked Alex. Arnold ambled away, and Ann, absolutely amazed ...

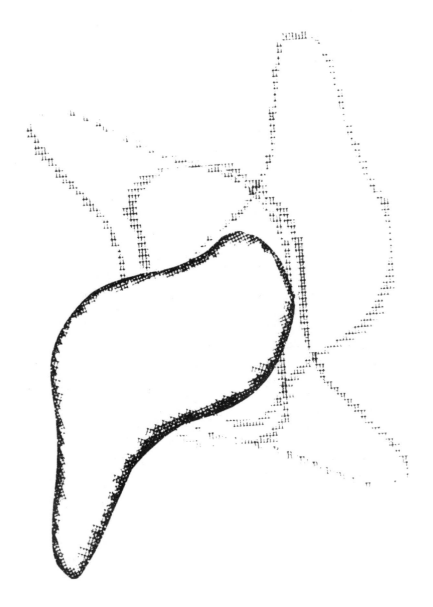

052273

probable systems 23

for Noam Chomsky

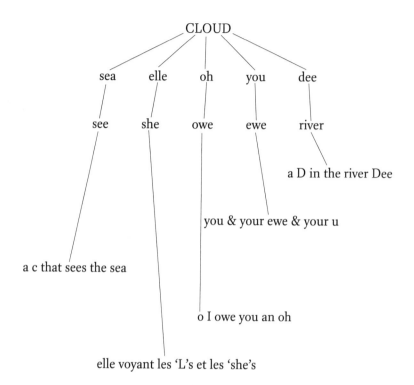

supper

apple

cider

cedar sea
(december 72)

see deer too
          or bear

memory

1969

private lines to
the interior

•

a pull
tugging at the heart

cheap image in heat
he sighs

        'dervish memory'

the same O re itself

the whole business

notes

        la

ti

•

lot T or A

i am back at
the cross
          roads

A: a deer

B: the trees

woods

a reading

physical contexts of human words

In a number of the preceding PROBABLE SYSTEMS, we have been examining concepts like 'the weight of speech,' 'the speed of thot,' etc. What becomes increasingly apparent is the need for certain world standards when it comes to print. Something as simple as measuring the circumference of words is made meaningless by the virtual babel of type-faces and type-sizes.

If a world standard were adopted – something like, say, 10 pt, or 12 pt, Helvetica, Garamond or Futura – then numerous variables could be taken into account & meaningful discussions & research could begin to take place. For instance, a more accurate notation of pitch and volume variables would become possible.* It could also illuminate discussion of the justified paragraph versus the preferred typographic mode of ragged right. And, of course, that old question of the time it takes for the mind to get around certain old thinking would finally be answerable.

This is merely to point to the advantages of setting up such a standard. Those interested could begin by forming local study groups to discuss the problem and approaches to be taken in order to get their government to adopt the notion of a World Standard for Print Size & Style. We can only hope that this initiative does not go the way of Esperanto.

written: Spring 1978
additional research & final draft: Summer 1988

---

* As an instance of what i'm saying here: pitch could be tracked through gradated use of type-faces; similarly, volume could be indicated by gradated use of type-sizes.

poem beginning with an old poem

addition

    i
add
   it on

no poem
Pope M

'po' poem'
rising

po po eem
po   em
  mmmmmmm
  mmmmmmm

mmmmmmmmmmmmmmmm
mmmmm m m m m m m m
             m   m
          m   m   m
        m   m
              m
   m   m   m   m
          m   m
   m
             m
        m
                m

          m

        m

mythopoesis

an oasis

an o as is

not a circle an elipse is ellipsis

o's mission

miss ion of 72
from me to you
april 73

p o e

M

d c c c c
I x x i i i
don't know

k's no w
that for sure

f/ or
s u r e

April 5

dreamed anthology 7

a poem by Gwendolyn MacEwan

I came into the grocery store
I walked in
–
–

He was standing by the counter
–
–
–

Him and his cronies
The six of them there
–
–

Like a bunch of ghosts
–
–
–

–
–
–
–

What do you think, Mr. Jones?
How long do you think, Mr. Jones?
Is it possible, Mr. Jones?
What about it, Mr. Jones?

– incomplete
title: 'The Ghosts'
January 9th, 1988

---

* In my dream I have been asked to read this poem of Gwen's at the Memorial Service for her. It's a multiple choice poem. There are six stanzas and each stanza gives the reader a choice of four lines to read. I am looking at this poem in a book and trying to figure out which line I should read for each stanza.

Negatives 2: Bridge Force

(for & after Frank Davey)

I

       shone
like

'm seated in my car
&
       travelled around the world
and just

           draws me

      out and on and

II

in its mouth

the image
the word
the letter

somehow, pleading with you

again

Mr. Conductor please
'fore my muscles freeze
I must get across
of course of course

they're all coming in fast

at last

III

, that pose,

supply

BETWEEN THE EYES

, tho not at once,

&

, caught tho he may be in his head,

believe me

closing his mouth &

, fell flat on his face

, believe me,

IV

time

by day
        at night

too

      as the skin clings
into/

      quarrel the year away
until –

    for love
of love   's love
of love's loving   's love

, still clinging

& nights

to look into

V
(ROAD TO JAPAN)

, the reader,

he is really

on

& feeling he's

floating above

finally

, word-filled man

VI

from here

moving inland

Forced by the facts of geography

anything detour
& still

(as in wood) you apply
to get the cut right
we have our own way of perceiving
as you did &

, in our world,
where we came &

peaceful,

& unimaginable

VII

                    there
even if you look up
            , an act of faith

searching the skies

                    other
staring at each

                            again

                        forming their own patterns

caught up in &

imagining another land
            reaching

there

this hell or this

peering up

tumbling round
         allows me to be
admitted
                                    where she sits or stands

                  , this motion,

         far distant or long ago

VIII

I sat here,

                                                    , to tell you of
                        , the ones who come as supplicants,
                              , & how they

           whom we have labelled

                 travellers, holy

                 crowds who
                 knock & knock again
                 as if to invoke
                              , the forms of gods,
           insistent in their ritual
                       are

IX

opens

i looked up thru

whom i have prayed to so often
i can almost see you

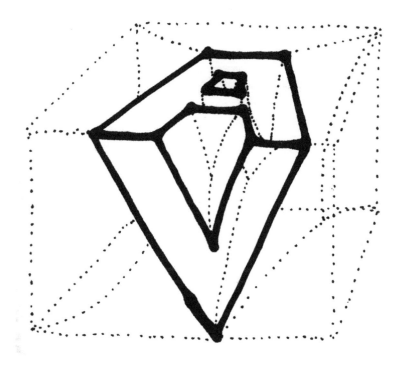

Kite 6
November 1972

CONTENT (with small press runs)

1

ink

(in like a lake)

fin flynn

        small connections

snail like
a lack of
S

   cargo nailed down

town

2

reader ship

& the wavering
up & down
200 to 500 to seven hundred

fifty and one
thou

sand and
sea

sail or
steam

sea/m

3

many or one 'r

any on board at all
points

forwards & backwards

type cast or
photographed

paging

4

hello

out there

reading me

listening with the third eye

hi

February 18th, 1981

Water Poem 5

probable systems 25

the empty place — some signs of the existence of anti-earth

PRELIMINARY NOTES:

apoetic
atheistic
asymbolic
asymmetrical
etc.

If 'a' as a prefix (from the Greek 'a-' (negative)) means, essentially, 'anti-',* is an opposite, then, logically, we are lead to the following:

EXAMPLES:

#1 – *aardvark* – the antithesis of ardvark. 'aarde' is the Dutch 'earth', & 'vark' a pig. but we already know that 'a', when placed as a prefix, means 'anti-'. hence 'aarde' (which should be understood as 'a-arde') means 'anti-earth', & 'aardvark' a pig from anti-earth. this betrays a knowledge of anti-earth (or 'a-earth') in the collective unconscious.

#2 – *aeon*, 'eon' & 'aeon' are acceptable variants in spelling the same word. it is easy to see then that, at least in the origin of the concept, 'time' & 'anti-time' (non-time?) were (are?) interchangeable concepts. the yin-yang balance of reality asserts itself. a-time (aeon) is part of aearth. just as time is part of earth.

#3 – *atheistic*, with its fascinating hint that the knowledge of aearth was banned, became seen as part of the devil's work (i.e. 'anti-theistic'), points, perhaps, to the historical explanation for consciousness of aearth becoming lost.**

---

* note, in what follows, that in the list of 'aa-' words the first 'a' is silent, a probable further proof of what i am saying here.
** see also 'PROBABLE SYSTEMS 10: a time machine', in the author's *ZYGAL: a book of mysteries & translations* (Coach House Press, Toronto, 1985). there is a probable connection between the points raised here and the conclusions reached in that earlier essay.

Earlier, in PROBABLE SYSTEMS 22, i spoke of 'the empty place' & its disappearance from language as we know it at the time of the break-up of the original mother tongue, the original unified system of signs. what better concept to describe 'aearth' than 'the empty place', that place where all that we know is no longer present, is empty of what is familiar, exists as a negative (a possible negation) of our own universe (& note that those two concepts tend to get confused). as already noted above, there was a shift that took place in which, for whatever reason, the existence of anti-earth was erased from the memory of the gene pool.

But among the hints that still point to its existence is the 'a': the 'a' which begins the alphabet (& begins our ability to speak of this reality); the 'a-' which negates this reality. 'a' is the bridge sign which links earth to aearth, the pivot between the realphabet** & the a-lphabet (or a-alphabet), and where we have to begin if we wish to truly begin.

A BEGINNING LIST OF OTHER VOCABULARY TO BE EXAMINED:

Aa – a stream, a water-course.

Aachen – a city on the border between W. Germany & Belgium.

Aak – an obsolete form of 'oak'.

Aal – a plant, allied to the madder, the roots of which yield a red dye.

Aalborg – a seaport in N. Jutland, Denmark.

Aalst – a city in West Central Belgium.

Aar (or Aare) – a river in Switzerland flowing into the Rhine.

---

* the concept of the 'realphabet' is discussed at length in 'PROBABLE SYSTEMS 14: rediscovery of the 22 letter alphabet, an archaeological report' (included in *Canadian "Pataphysics* (edited by the Toronto Research Group, Underwhich Editions, Toronto, 1980).

Aardwolf – an African mammal resembling a hyena but feeding chiefly on termites & larvae.

Aargau – a canton (state) in N. Switzerland.

Aarhus – a seaport in E. Jutland, Denmark.

Aaron – the older brother of Moses and first high priest of the Hebrews.

Ab – the 11th month of the Jewish year (i.e. November).

Abadon – the place of the dead, the nether world.

Another – often 'a nother' = a second, a remaining, a different.

Aune – an ell; an obsolete French cloth measure which varied in length in different localities.

Aunsetter – an obsolete form of 'ancestor'.

Aunsion – an obsolete form of 'ancient'.

written: 1974 to 1976
additional research and final draft: Summer 1988

dreamed anthology 8

a poem by Victor Coleman

cars

-swish-

in the

streets

-swish-

-swish-

– fragment only
UNTITLED:

August 22nd, 1988

---

in my dream i am talking to Victor about how this poem reminds me of one by Gerry Gilbert, particularly the part remembered here. Victor tells me the poem (some two pages in length) is incomplete without the sculpture it is meant to accompany, and he points to a Jean-Tinguely-style machine/sculpture he is sitting next to and, throwing a switch, activates it. a number of wheels in the sculpture begin to turn and Victor relates that motion to the section of the poem we are talking about.

toadality

For you i kill ya.
coz o' you to become you.
miss you? not at all!

bashaiku

fronds.
old
pond-
cold-

a
frog
jumps from a
log.

in
water
things
stir
     -PLINK
KER

a short story (for Lionel Kearns 8 years later)

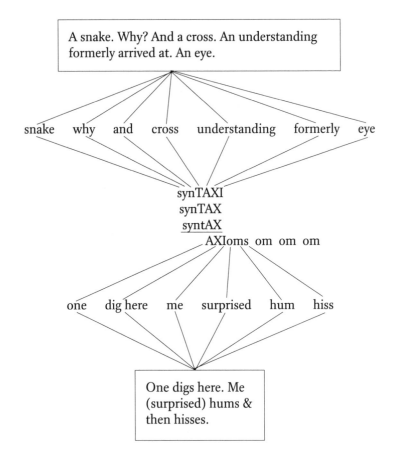

> A snake. Why? And a cross. An understanding
> formerly arrived at. An eye.

snake   why   and   cross   understanding   formerly   eye

synTAXI
synTAX
syntAX
AXIoms om om om

one   dig here   me   surprised   hum   hiss

> One digs here. Me
> (surprised) hums &
> then hisses.

November 1974–April 1976

Negatives 6: who moves

(for & after Daphne Marlatt)

i

moves
to use

play

mirage
molten
go down

what was once absence

her

ii
lack of

iii

in or
the

and the
bleeds

away turn

out of sight

moonlight

of a sudden

iv

that this

personal
visible, scarcely

love

shines

v

wait in

tension

go into

I do.

The Actual Life of Language 3

Frog Pond turns into a gold mine

Toronto Daily Star
August 19th, 1988

052573

afterword

for Robert Duncan

and now that you are gone
now that you are gone
that you are gone
you are gone
are gone
gone
one
on
o

The last poem in bpNichol's final notebook
Sept. 12/88

The Editor's Acknowledgements

My sincere thanks goes to Coach House, who are Alana Wilcox, Evan Munday, Leigh Nash, Heidi Waechtler, Stan Bevington and Rick/ Simon for their time, commitment and support for this project. Thanks to Justin Stephenson for his breathtaking cover design and to Peter Ballestrieri for his meticulous copyediting.

I offer my gratitude to Kevin Williams at Talonbooks and Charles Alexander at Chax Press for permission to republish *love: a book of remembrances* (1974) and *art facts: a book of contexts* (1990) respectively. Thanks to Lori Emerson and Darren Wershler for contributing their biography of Nichol.

I would also like to thank the numerous people who offered their time, energy, generosity and expertise: angela rawlings, Jennifer Wolfe, Shannon Meek, Adalaide Morris, Nathan Brown, Michael Ondaatje, Charles Bernstein, Robyn Schiff, James Papoutsis, Christian Bök, Jason Demers, Justin Voyce, the staff in Special Collections and Rare Books at Simon Fraser University, and the Digital Studio for the Public Humanities at the University of Iowa.

Finally, I'd like to recognize and thank Ellie Nichol for her permission to undertake this project and for her warm encouragement throughout.

Stephen Voyce is Assistant Professor of English and a member of the Digital Studio for the Public Humanities at the University of Iowa.

He is the author of *Poetic Community: Avant-Garde Activism and Cold War Culture* (University of Toronto Press, 2013) and the Director of the Fluxus Digital Collection (UI Libraries/DSPH). Voyce teaches courses on contemporary literature, twentieth-century poetics and media studies.

His work also appears in journals such as *Modernism/modernity, Criticism: A Quarterly Journal for Literature and the Arts, Postmodern Culture* and *Open Letter*.

bpNichol (Barrie Phillip Nichol) was born September 30, 1944, in Vancouver, British Columbia. He died in Toronto, Ontario, on September 25, 1988.

Nichol's writing is, by definition, engaged with a phenomenon he called 'borderblur': in his lifetime he wrote (somewhere between) poetry, novels, short fiction, children's books, musical scores, comic book art, collage/assemblage and computer texts. Nichol was also an inveterate collaborator, working with the sound poetry ensemble The Four Horsemen (Nichol, Rafael Barreto-Rivera, Paul Dutton and Steve McCaffery); with Steve McCaffery as part of the Toronto Research Group (TRG); with the visual artist Barbara Caruso; and with countless other writers.

Nichol also had (and continues to have) a large presence on screens of various sizes. In the mid-1980s, he became a writer for the children's television show *Fraggle Rock*, produced by Jim Henson. His early work in sound was documented in Michael Ondaatje's short film *Sons of Captain Poetry*. A second full-length film on Nichol, *bp: pushing the boundaries*, directed by Brian Nash, was completed in the 1990s. Nichol also appears in Ron Mann's film *Poetry in Motion*.

Though Nichol's initial attempts at writing in the early 1960s produced fiction and lyric poetry, he first garnered international attention with his hand-drawn concrete and visual poems. These texts work brilliantly against the conventions of the traditional lyric poem by exploring the material, tangible and aural qualities of the word and the letter. (Not surprisingly, Nichol's work with the aural qualities of language led him to sound poetry, resulting in the release of four solo audio recordings.)

Nichol's first major collection of concrete poetry, *Konfessions of an Elizbethan Fan Dancer*, marked the beginning of a long engagement with the typewriter and its unique ability to mechanically reproduce letters an exact distance apart. In other words, the grid-like qualities of typewritten text allowed Nichol to create meaning semantically and horizontally as well as visually and vertically. Soon after, Nichol was boxing and publishing loose pages of concrete in *bp, Still Water* and an edited collection, *The Cosmic Chef: An Evening of Concrete*. While Nichol's concrete poems illustrate an astonishing range of techniques and concerns, other early works such as *ABC: the aleph beth book* and *Aleph Unit* point to his lifelong interest in representing process by gradually transforming series of letter-shapes.

Exemplifying the dictum spelled out in the 'Statement' printed on the back of *bp* that 'there are no barriers in art,' Nichol won the 1970 Governor General's Award for poetry with not one but four publications: the prose booklet *The True Eventual Story of Billy the Kid*, the collection of lyric poems *Beach Head*, the boxed concrete sequence *Still Water* and *The Cosmic Chef*, a boxed anthology of concrete and visual poetry.

It was partly through his work with concrete poetry in sequences such as the one in *Extreme Positions* that Nichol discovered innovative ways to work with narrative. Nichol reworked and remixed the conventions of the novel, the western, the detective story, the romance, the diary and the autobiography. The results included the deconstructive metafiction of *The True Eventual Story of Billy the Kid*; the mad jumble of prose poetry, seedy sexploitation, personal and historical letters, science fiction and cartoons that is *Two Novels*; the stream-of-consciousness of *Journal*; the autobiographical accounts of Nichol's vagina, tonsils, lungs and other vital bits in *Selected Organs*; and so on.

Nichol continued to subvert formal and thematic conventions in his shorter poems and sequences. He moved effortlessly between genres, blurring and experimenting with generic boundaries to produce writing as varied as the minimalist lyricism of *The Other Side of the Room*; the pun-filled, semantically complex *Journeying & the Returns*; the translations of translations of (who else?) Apollinaire in *Translating Translating Apollinaire*.

The series of books that began with *love: a book of remembrances* and was followed by *zygal: a book of mysteries and translations*, *art facts: a book of contexts*, and the posthumous *Truth: a book of fictions* was an ideal means for Nichol to continue developing a number of poem sequences. These range from his concrete letter poems to the series 'probable systems,' 'I.T.A.N.U.T.S.' and 'Studies in the Book Machine.' Most readers and critics see Nichol's *The Martyrology* not only as the culmination of all of his work but as one of the most important long poems of the twentieth century. Begun in 1967 and remaining unfinished at the time of his death in 1988, *The Martyrology* is an open-ended, lifelong poem that endlessly problematizes issues of textuality, reading and writing.

Given Nichol's dedication to the process of writing, it should come as no surprise that the form of *The Martyrology* underwent countless transformations over the years – writing, rewriting and expanding on previous books, formally and thematically inventing and reinventing itself and its pantheon of linguistic 'saints' (words beginning with the letters 'st') over and over again. For example, the section 'Clouds' from Book 2, which continues to explore the mythology of the saints first introduced in Book 1, is brought back as the ghostly presence of Book 5's 'Chain 11' – Nichol has systematically taken out most of the words and left only clusters of certain letters. As Nichol said of *The Martyrology* in 1987, 'This text has not closed.'

Typeset in Goluska and Classic Grotesque

The Goluska typeface was designed by Canadian type designer Rod McDonald to honour his long-time friend Glenn Goluska, 1947–2011. Goluska was one of Canada's finest designers who had a lifelong love for the work of the noted American typographer and type designer William Addison Dwiggins. The typeface Goluska is a homage to Dwiggins' famous typeface, Electra. Although McDonald tried to capture some of the feel of Electra, he avoided making a slavish copy. Goluska is sturdier and the x-height is larger than Electra.

The Monotype Grotesque typefaces were among the first sans serifs cut for hot-metal machine typesetting. Rod McDonald describes them as 'hidden gems that deserved to be updated.' First released in 1926, the origins of the Grotesques can be traced back to two virtually forgotten German typefaces: the Venus and Ideal Grotesk designs. In 2008, Monotype gave him the go-ahead to draw what would become the Classic Grotesque family.

Printed at the old Coach House on bpNichol Lane in Toronto, Ontario, on Zephyr Antique Laid paper, which was manufactured, acid-free, in Saint-Jérôme, Quebec, from second-growth forests. This book was printed with vegetable-based ink on a 1965 Heidelberg KORD offset litho press. Its pages were folded on a Baumfolder, gathered by hand, bound on a Sulby Auto-Minabinda and trimmed on a Polar single-knife cutter.

Edited for the press by Stephen Voyce
Designed by Alana Wilcox
Cover design by Justin Stephenson
Photo of Stephen Voyce by Barry Phipps
Photo of bpNichol by David Hlynsky

Coach House Books
80 bpNichol Lane
Toronto ON M5S 3J4
Canada

416 979 2217
800 367 6360

mail@chbooks.com
www.chbooks.com

819
.154
Nicho

Nichol, B.
A book of variations.
Aurora P.L. NOV13
33164005096941